Learning Oriented A

A systemic approach

For a complete list of titles please visit: www.cambridge.org/elt/silt

Also in this series:

Learning Oriented Assessment

A systemic approach

Neil Jones
Consultant, Cambridge English Language Assessment

and

Nick Saville
Cambridge English Language Assessment

With input from
Angeliki Salamoura
Cambridge English Language Assessment

CAMBRIDGE
UNIVERSITY PRESS

CAMBRIDGE
UNIVERSITY PRESS

University Printing House, Cambridge CB2 8BS, United Kingdom

Cambridge University Press is part of the University of Cambridge.

It furthers the University's mission by disseminating knowledge in the pursuit of education, learning and research at the highest international levels of excellence.

www.cambridge.org
Information on this title: www.cambridge.org/9781316507889

First published 2016

A catalogue record for this publication is available from the British Library

Library of Congress Cataloging-in-Publication Data
Names: Jones, Neil, Dr., author. | Saville, Nick, editor. | University of
   Cambridge. Local Examinations Syndicate.
Title: Learning oriented assessment : a systemic approach / Neil Jones and
   Nick Saville.
Description: Cambridge ; New York : Cambridge English, [2016] | Series:
   Studies in language testing ; 45 | Includes bibliographical references and
   index.
Identifiers: LCCN 2016000619 | ISBN 9781316507889 (paperback)
Subjects: LCSH: Language and languages--Examinations. | Language and
   languages--Europe. | Education, Higher--Evaluation. | Educational tests
   and measurement. | Communication in education. | Language--Examinations |
   Europe--Languages.
Classification: LCC P53.4 .J66 2016 | DDC 418.0076--dc23 LC record available at http://lccn.loc.
gov/2016000619

To all the learners we have taught from 1970 to 2015

Contents

List of tables and figures

Abbreviations

ACTFL   American Council on the Teaching of Foreign Languages
ARG   Assessment Reform Group
CA   Cognitive Acceleration
CASE   Cognitive Acceleration through Science Education
CASP   Complex Adaptive System Principles
CBA   Classroom-based Assessment
CDA   Cognitive Diagnosis Approaches
CEFR   Common European Framework of Reference for Languages
CJ   Comparative Judgement
CT   Complexity Theory
ECD   Evidence-centred Design
ESLC   European Survey on Language Competences
ETS   Educational Testing Service
IRT   Item Response Theory
LAD   Language Acquisition Device
LFM   Learning for Mastery
LTT   Latent Trait Theory
MiL   Minimise Learning Effort
MOOC   Massive Open Online Course
NCATE   National Council for Accreditation of Teacher Education
PIAAC   Programme for the International Assessment of Adult
        Competencies
PIRLS   Progress in International Reading Literacy Study
PISA   Programme for International Student Assessment
PPP   Presentation, Practice, Performance
PSI   Personalized System of Instruction
SBA   School-based Assessment
SLA   Second Language Acquisition
TBA   Teacher-based Assessment
TIMSS   Trends in International Mathematics and Science Study
TLRP   Teaching and Learning Research Programme
VRIP   Validity, Reliability, Impact and Practicality

Acknowledgements

The authors would like to thank the following groups and individuals: Angeliki Salamoura, who worked closely with the authors, and for her expertise in Second Language Acquisition (SLA), psycholinguistics and the English Profile Programme, which fed into several chapters; Michael Milanovic, for his encouragement and support in writing the volume; Cyril Weir, for reading several proofs and his insightful comments on the content; Michael Carrier and Ted Briscoe, for their ideas on the use of technology to support learning in the ways presented in this volume; Miranda Hamilton, consultant to Cambridge English from 2010 to 2014, for her help in compiling the literature review and collating many of the ideas that have fed into this volume; the Asset Languages development team, for their attempt to implement an early version of the Learning Oriented Assessment approach over the period 2002 to 2013; colleagues in Cambridge English working on the concept of Impact by Design and its associated research agenda, for their input on this topic; members of Cambridge English who have implemented Learning Oriented Assessment-related ideas in their testing programmes over many years; the Cambridge English/Cambridge University Press team contributing to the Empower project, who have implemented the Learning Oriented Assessment approach; John Trim, for his wisdom in numerous conversations with the authors about the CEFR and its uses over many years, especially over the period 2001 to 2012; Jim Purpura, for wide-ranging discussions with Nick Saville on learning-oriented approaches to assessment dating back nearly two decades; Cyril Weir, Barry O'Sullivan, Lynda Taylor and many colleagues in Cambridge English, for collaborating with the authors on the development of the socio-cognitive approach over many years; the many teachers who took part in webinars and other Learning Oriented Assessment-related events at conferences where these ideas have been presented; participants at the American Association for Applied Linguistics 2013 symposium 'Learning Oriented Assessment (LOA) in Classrooms: A Place where SLA, Interaction, and Language Assessment Interface', organised by Jim Purpura and Nick Saville, who commented on the paper by Neil Jones, Miranda Hamilton and Nick Saville that was presented by the authors of this volume; participants at the Teachers College Columbia symposium in October 2014, who commented on the paper by Nick Saville and Angeliki Salamoura, 'Learning Oriented Assessment – A Systemic View from an Examination Provider' – in particular Sian Morgan for feedback on this manuscript; readers of the manuscript during the peer review process, especially Constant Leung and John Norris, for their insightful comments; members of Cambridge English staff, especially Stephen McKenna, for reading and commenting on a White Paper on Learning Oriented Assessment that preceded the full text of this volume; to Dylan Wiliam, for his kind permission to use Table 7.1 on page 82; and, finally, to John Savage, for his guidance and proofreading skills in preparing the text for publication.

Series Editors' note

This volume on Learning Oriented Assessment is timely in bringing together in one place a number of strands of thinking that have been running through developments in language assessment over the past 25 years. These strands have one point in common: an interest in the extent to which assessment promotes or hinders successful learning outcomes.

Although the authors are not alone in using the learning-oriented label to apply to their work, the approach adopted in this volume is distinct in that it provides a systemic overview that seeks to weave the various strands together into a coherent whole. It is this systemic dimension that, in their terms, provides a theory of action to bring about change and improve educational outcomes.

One of the early underpinning strands in this overview is the concept of test washback – the effect that external assessment has on teaching and learning in schools and in classroom contexts. Such matters have indeed been a concern of Cambridge English Language Assessment for a long time. Spolsky (2004:305) describes how:

> ... from its beginning UCLES [as Cambridge English Language Assessment was formerly known] accepted the key role to be played in test development by the "stakeholders" in particular those schools in various countries of the world that wished to establish examination centres, mainly for their own students. From the earliest years, the Cambridge test writers and their various committees saw themselves as sharing with the schools not so much an examination as the culmination of a teaching process. Before the word "backwash" had been coined, they regularly asked whether modifications being proposed in the form of the examination would be accepted by the schools.

It is clear that, historically, the starting point for UCLES had always been the educational context and how the examination might encourage the best practice in teaching in that context. The positive washback of its examinations on what was taught in the classroom was critical for UCLES. The examinations had always been characterised by a close relationship with pedagogy, i.e. curriculum, syllabus, classroom practice and the teaching profession. For example, the Executive Committee of UCLES in 1965 noted: 'the need for more precise information on the function of the examinations and their relationship with the curriculum and teaching they encourage', and, similarly, the British Council Cambridge Joint Committee (July 1968):

... underlined the need for research and progressive development in the English examinations with due consideration of the sort of teaching which is to be encouraged.

As Bachman, Davidson, Ryan and Choi (1995:131) observed in the first ever volume in the Studies in Language Testing (SiLT) series:

... the British examinations system is particularly concerned with promoting positive effects of examinations on curricula and instruction, and thus is sensitive to including features in its examinations that are consistent with those found in instructional programs.

Contemporary interest in washback really comes to life in the 1980s, when the communicative approach to teaching and testing began to take hold (Hawkey 2004). At that time it was not uncommon to hear comments from language teachers suggesting that examinations can have a positive washback on their teaching. In other words, the format and content of the test was also useful in their classroom teaching: for example, if the examination included a productive speaking test, it was helpful in structuring the teaching and learning of speaking in the classroom.

However, the idea that high-stakes examinations could also exert negative washback and actually hinder learning also began to emerge at that time. Examinations based on multiple-choice items were often taken as an example of test formats that encouraged cramming or test-wise behaviour rather than productive learning. It became clear that washback processes were actually poorly understood and not supported by empirical research. In fact, washback has proved to be a much more complex phenomenon than first thought and the thinking and research that has developed around it in the last 25 years has led to a rich literature. Several of the volumes in the SiLT series have provided an important contribution to this debate (Cheng 2005, Wall 2005, Green 2007).

In the course of that debate, the concept has also been extended to focus on the wider effects and consequences that assessment has in society. These days, impact and impact research encompass washback (see Hawkey 2004) but also go well beyond the school context to deal with the macro issues, such as policy-based reform projects that affect the whole educational 'ecosystem'. This latter point emerges as a key feature of the Learning Oriented Assessment system.

The notion of positive 'impact by design' forms an important part of the systemic view presented in this volume. This accords with the increased attention being given to the social dimension of assessment in language testing circles – rather than the more technical and psychometric concerns which predated Messick's seminal work on validity (1989).

In some parts of the world, educational movements emerged in the 1990s which questioned the role of large-scale testing programmes in formal education and sought to put more emphasis on classroom-based assessment, with teachers playing a central role. The Assessment Reform Group, with its focus on formative assessment (Assessment for Learning), is a good example of this in the UK context.

Central to such movements has been a call to change the approach to assessment in order to raise educational standards and improve achievement in schools. In language testing this call has led to a need for improved measurement scales which can be used to assess progression more accurately and interpretive frameworks to report the outcomes of learning to stakeholders, for example in simple-to-understand 'can do' terminology.

The most influential of such frameworks is the Common European Framework of Reference for Languages (CEFR) (Council of Europe 2001) which provides the basis for developing assessment scales across the proficiency continuum and for promoting good practice in language teaching and learning focusing on the core construct of communicative language ability. In the Learning Oriented Assessment approach the role of an interpretative framework is central and the authors use the CEFR as a particularly useful example (see Martyniuk (Ed) 2010 on CEFR issues).

Another strand which picks up on this point has been the questioning of what we understand by language learning, and how formal approaches to learning a language can be treated as a unique case of learning more generally. The body of research in the area of language acquisition has provided a useful starting point in thinking about these questions but in keeping with the other socially oriented movements noted above, constructivist principles have emerged as the front runner in providing possible answers.

At the heart of this is not only how to approach the task of teaching and learning but also what has to be learned. In the case of the authors of this volume, they are mainly concerned with English as a second or additional language in contexts where the learners already know at least one and sometimes two other languages (e.g. the home language and the language of schooling). This points to a need for richer descriptions of English as a target language and for research into the ways that specific types of assessment and feedback at different levels of proficiency promote successful learning.

Fundamentally this is a multilingual challenge so it is important to understand how English should be presented to learners at different stages of their learning journey throughout their lifespan and to understand how their prior learning of other languages hinders or helps this. In this respect, the authors cite important work which has been conducted using learner data which might point to better ways of individualising learning and assessing progress – see the English Profile Studies series (Hawkins and Filipović 2012, Green 2012, Ćatibušić and Little 2014, North 2014, Harrison and Barker (Eds) 2015) and the 'construct volumes' in the SiLT series (Shaw and Weir 2007, Khalifa and Weir 2009, Taylor (Ed) 2011, Geranpayeh and Taylor (Eds) 2013).

In bringing together the systemic approach to Learning Oriented Assessment and in focusing on the various contexts of learning in society, the authors also address the question of change and change processes. How can improvements be implemented and outcome achievements measured more effectively?

The authors' use of quotations from John Dewey throughout the volume remind us that this challenge has eluded even some of the most eminent scholars and educationalists in the past. But 12 years after the launch of Facebook, the potentially transformative opportunity that offers hope for progress is the pervasive use of mobile technology – and a generation of learners who are completely comfortable in using the small screen to organise their lives.

The challenge now is to capitalise on this opportunity in order to implement the systemic approach and bring about the changes that are called for.

References

Bachman, L F, Davidson, F, Ryan, K and Choi, I-C (1995) *An Investigation into the Comparability of Two Tests of English as a Foreign Language,* Studies in Language Testing volume 1, Cambridge: UCLES/Cambridge University Press.

Ćatibušić, B and Little, D (2014) *Immigrant Pupils Learn English: A CEFR-related Study of Empirical Development*, English Profile Studies volume 3, Cambridge: UCLES/Cambridge University Press.

Cheng L (2005) *Changing Language Teaching through Language Testing: A Washback Study*, Studies in Language Testing volume 21, Cambridge: UCLES/Cambridge University Press.

Council of Europe (2001) *Common European Framework of Reference for Languages: Learning, Teaching, Assessment*, Cambridge: Cambridge University Press.

Geranpayeh, A and Taylor, L (Eds) (2013) *Examining Listening: Research and Practice in Assessing Second Language Listening,* Studies in Language Testing volume 35, Cambridge: UCLES/Cambridge University Press.

Green, A (2007) *IELTS Washback in Context: Preparation for Academic Writing in Higher Education*, Studies in Language Testing volume 25, Cambridge: UCLES/Cambridge University Press.

Green, A (2012) *Language Functions Revisited: Theoretical and Empirical Bases Across the Ability Range*, English Profile Studies volume 2, Cambridge: UCLES/Cambridge University Press.

Harrison, J and Barker, F (Eds) (2015) *English Profile in Practice*, English Profile Studies volume 5, Cambridge: UCLES/Cambridge University Press.

Hawkey, R (2004) *A Modular Approach to Testing English Language Skills: The Development of the Certificates in English Language Skills (CELS) Examinations,* Studies in Language Testing volume 16, Cambridge: UCLES/Cambridge University Press.

Hawkins, J A and Filipović, L (2012) *Criterial Features in L2 English: Specifying the Reference Levels of the Common European Framework*, English Profile Studies volume 1, Cambridge: UCLES/Cambridge University Press.

Khalifa, H and Weir, C J (2009) *Examining Reading: Research and Practice in Assessing Second Language Reading*, Studies in Language Testing volume 29, Cambridge: UCLES/Cambridge University Press.

Martyniuk, W (Ed) (2010) *Aligning Tests with the CEFR: Reflections on using the Council of Europe's draft Manual*, Studies in Language Testing volume 33, Cambridge: UCLES/Cambridge University Press.

Messick, S A (1989) Validity, in Linn, R L (Ed) *Educational Measurement* (3rd edition), New York: Macmillan, 13–103.

North, B (2014) *The CEFR in Practice*, English Profile Studies volume 4, Cambridge: UCLES/Cambridge University Press.

Shaw, S and Weir, C J (2007) *Examining Writing: Research and Practice in Assessing Second Language Writing*, Studies in Language Testing volume 26, Cambridge: UCLES/Cambridge University Press.

Spolsky, B (2004) Review: Continuity and innovation: Revising the Cambridge Proficiency in English Examination 1913–2002, *ELT Journal* 58 (3), 305–309.

Taylor, L (Ed) (2011) *Examining Speaking: Research and Practice in Assessing Second Language Speaking*, Studies in Language Testing volume 30, Cambridge: UCLES/Cambridge University Press.

Wall, D (2005) *The Impact of High-stakes Testing on Classroom Teaching: A Case Study Using Insights from Testing and Innovation Theory*, Studies in Language Testing volume 22, Cambridge: UCLES/Cambridge University Press.

1 Learning Oriented Assessment: An overview

'It requires troublesome work to undertake the alteration of old beliefs.'

How We Think (John Dewey 1933:29–30)

Learning a language is one of the first things we do in life. It is a natural and wholly engaging process. However, approaches to the formal teaching of language have in many contexts made it an unnatural, frustrating and remarkably inefficient one. Evidence for this was provided by the European Survey on Language Competences (ESLC) in 2012. In half of the 16 participating jurisdictions, about half of the students or more achieved only Common European Framework of References for Languages (CEFR) Level A1 in the first foreign language at the end of lower secondary education, or failed to achieve even that. To have spent up to six years of study to achieve so little indicates that in many countries something is seriously wrong in language education.

Assessment is also a natural process, and one intimately connected with learning. Think of the expression 'learning by experience': it denotes a largely unconscious process in which some task is engaged with, the outcomes are noted and evaluated, and the experience provides feedback on how to do better next time. This basic cycle – task performance, observation, evaluation and feedback – is common to all assessment, of one's own performance or of others, formal or informal. But educational assessment, particularly as conducted through the mechanisms of large-scale standardised testing, has become systematised in ways which, even where they are intended to promote learning, often fail to do so effectively. The country which performed worst of all in the ESLC went on to achieve results in a national exam the following summer which on paper appeared creditable, and which were indeed acclaimed as 'impressive' by a language teachers' association. Clearly, the communicative language competence which the ESLC set out to measure is not what these students were learning, or what their exam was testing.

We could do better. Learning Oriented Assessment as presented in this volume offers a vision of radical change and far more effective learning. It is written from the perspective of an assessment body, but it looks to both formal assessment and classroom assessment, seeking to exploit the synergies between them: it is *systemic*.

There are two key purposes of assessment: to promote learning, and to measure and interpret what has been learned. In some contexts additional duties are imposed on assessment, notably that of holding schools to account for their performance. This has been observed to work against achievement of the key purposes, because it provides 'perverse incentives' for schools to teach to the test, to the detriment of learning. This identifies a further feature of Learning Oriented Assessment: it must be *ecological*, ensuring that all aspects of the system work in harmony to serve the most important goals.

The twin goals of promoting and measuring learning have been characterised as *formative* and *summative* respectively, but this familiar distinction is one which Learning Oriented Assessment must challenge, because it represents these two purposes as fundamentally at odds with each other. A systemic and ecological approach seeks complementarity: informal classroom assessment and formal large-scale assessment should both contribute to the two key purposes of assessment: to provide evidence *of* learning and evidence *for* learning.

Learning Oriented Assessment is presented in Figure 1.1 in terms of two complementary dimensions. Large-scale, standardised assessment provides the vertical dimension, describing progression through lower to higher levels of proficiency. It is primarily *quantitative*, addressing the question: *how far have students progressed?* But in answering that question it must do more than simply rank students from better to worse – that is the quickest way to demotivate students and lead them to adopt defective learning strategies. What is crucial is that it should provide an *interpretation* of performance, which directs the attention of students, teachers and society in general towards the important goals of language learning. The CEFR levels shown in Figure 1.1 represent that vital interpretive framework.

The horizontal dimension depicts the *qualitative* differences between learners, addressing the question: *how can each learner be helped to progress?* It groups learners who are all at the same global proficiency level but differ in terms of their cognition, their experience, and their learning needs. Understanding students' particular characteristics is essential to individualising teaching and learning.

The vertical, quantitative dimension is the primary domain of assessment experts, if only because the construction and interpretation of a scale of language proficiency is a highly technical issue. The horizontal, qualitative dimension is the primary domain of the classroom and the teacher. But there is complementarity and overlap. Quantitative evidence can help identify the skills profiles of individual learners, as well as their current overall level. Qualitative evidence promotes learning gains that are reflected in quantitative measures. Positive evidence of learning motivates students to further learning.

The aim of this systemic model of Learning Oriented Assessment is not to promote test-based teaching or impose more large-scale assessment on

Figure 1.1 A complementary relationship between large-scale and classroom assessment

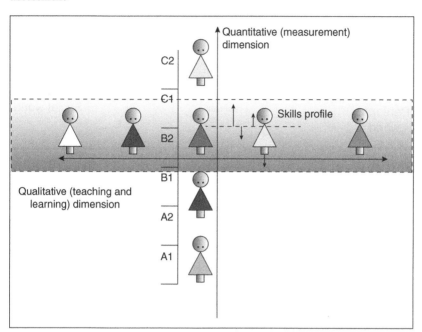

the classroom – an unwelcome recent trend in many contexts – but rather to define fully complementary, coherent roles for the expertise of teachers and assessment professionals, providing a supporting framework for learning, but where essential responsibilities still remain with teachers and students in the classroom. Implementing Learning Oriented Assessment as presented here is a task for both educationalists and assessment experts.

Another systemic view is offered by Figure 1.2, which shows 'four worlds' of learning: the personal world, concerned with the individual's developing cognition; the social world, which rewards the acquisition of both social and professional language skills; the world of education, which organises learning into subjects and curriculum objectives; and the world of assessment, whose task is essentially to link the other worlds together, by providing constructs of language ability which enable meaningful measurement of learners, documentation of skills which are of value in the social world, targets for schools to achieve through their teaching, and evidence of how effective that teaching has been.

In other words, it is assessment which is able to bring the other worlds together, enabling them to pursue common goals which have social value. This may be seen as its proper role.

Figure 1.2 Four worlds of learning

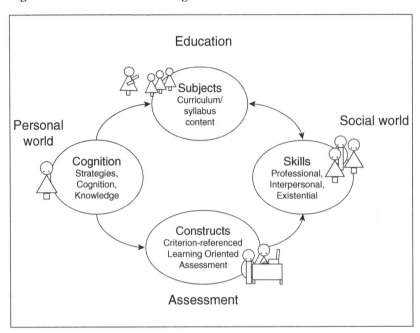

Common goals require a common focus. Figure 1.3 links the worlds through a learning cycle based on the performance of a task, observation, and feedback.

Tasks are placed at the centre because they have relevance to each of the worlds. They provide a context for classroom exercises and an approach to organising formal education. The social world values skilled performance on tasks. The individual's cognition, as we will explain, develops through engagement with tasks. Assessment uses tasks as the basis of measures.

Putting tasks at the centre is not primarily a methodological claim (although as presented in section 3.3.1, tasks are a basic element in organising teaching), but rather highlights the importance for the cognitive development of learners of engagement in meaningful communication, and, what follows, the practical utility of tasks for aligning the different worlds around a common focus which has social value.

Figure 1.3 shows tasks leading to learning in two ways: through natural acquisition by engaging with tasks in the real world, as well as through the route of formal learning. That natural acquisition may play a part in an individual's second language learning is, again, not primarily a methodological claim, but further underlines the primacy of meaningful communication.

Figure 1.3 is returned to in Chapter 8, where it plays an important part in

Figure 1.3 The four worlds linked by a focus on task

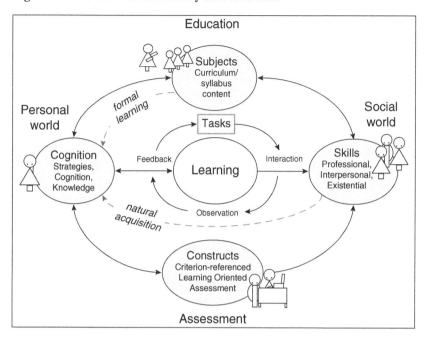

presenting our approach to aligning classroom and assessment data in order to fulfil the twin goals of Learning Oriented Assessment: to provide evidence *of* learning and *for* learning.

The purpose of this volume is not to provide detailed prescriptions for classroom activities (even if some readers may be disappointed by this). Rather, it sets out from a theoretical perspective, with the aim of developing a coherent model of how assessment can impact positively on learning, based on a broad exploration of the literature on learning and assessment. To add structure we will present findings as answers to three fundamental questions:

- What is learning? This addresses the personal world, individual cognition.
- What is to be learned? This addresses organised education, and how it meets the needs of society.
- What is the role of assessment in learning? This addresses the complementary roles of large-scale assessment and classroom assessment.

The answers to these questions will support claims for how all levels of assessment can be made to work together to achieve radically better learning outcomes.

What is the intended audience for this volume? We hope it will contribute firstly to discussion within the language assessment community of how their role within education should develop in future. Thus it is also a kind of manifesto, hopefully of interest to those who directly use assessment services. But above all the volume targets the wider audience who have a professional or personal interest in the issue of education and how better to make it serve its role in society.

1.1 The organisation of this volume

This chapter sets out in summary the argument for Learning Oriented Assessment, entailing a number of claims and assertions which will not be immediately supported, though references are provided to subsequent chapters, where each aspect of the argument is treated in detail. The intention is to lay out the key elements of Learning Oriented Assessment, and provide signposting to the later chapters. This approach means that some material in this chapter is repeated and expanded upon in the later ones.

Chapter 2 sets the scene by providing a historical account of how learning-oriented concepts of assessment have developed in a range of contexts and in response to a range of issues.

Chapter 8 is the point towards which the text leads, as it draws together from the earlier chapters a model that aligns large-scale assessment and classroom learning-oriented assessment around shared goals and a common interpretive framework.

Finally, Chapter 9 brings the volume to a close by considering various issues of implementation to be addressed by Learning Oriented Assessment: educational policy-making, lessons from the formative assessment literature and the Asset Languages project, and the crucial role of technology. It also presents a case study of the impact of Cambridge English exams in a particular context, which is included to indicate how the monitoring and evaluation of Learning Oriented Assessment may be undertaken. The last section of Chapter 9 offers a conclusion.

This volume presents a model of learning-oriented assessment developed by Cambridge English Language Assessment, an exam board within Cambridge Assessment, which is part of the University of Cambridge. The model is referred to in the text as Learning Oriented Assessment (with initial capitals). In this text the term 'Cambridge English' is used as shorthand for Cambridge English Language Assessment.

The quotations that head each chapter are taken from the writings of John Dewey (1859–1952), the American philosopher, psychologist and educational reformer. In Shepard's (2000:12) presentation of social constructivism she comments that 'John Dewey anticipated all of these ideas 100 years ago.' Norris (2009, 2015) also recognises Dewey's influence. The quotations are a reminder that while the proposals in this volume have the authority that comes with age, they also present challenges that have defeated the best efforts of several generations. But we will argue in our conclusions that Learning Oriented Assessment is an idea whose time has finally come.

1.2 What is learning?

This section largely summarises Chapter 3, and at its centre is the learner.

1.2.1 Social constructivism

It is important for the argument to be developed in this text that we should adopt an explicit model of learning. The model which Learning Oriented Assessment adopts is a *social constructivist* one (see section 3.1). Social constructivism sees learning and meaning-making as an intrinsically social process. Learning is dialogue. It proceeds within communities of discourse and practice, and learning is mediated through the shared practices of the community: the tools, signs, models, methods and theories which they construct. A classroom is a community of practice, and so is each school subject.

Social constructivism may be distinguished from cognitive constructivism. The latter focuses on the nature of an individual's cognition and is associated with the work of Piaget (1896–1980), while the emphasis on the social context of cognitive development is associated with the work of Vygotsky (1896–1934). These are differences of emphasis within an overall conception of *situated cognition,* which places the development of individual cognition within the larger physical and social context of interactions (see section 3.1.1).

Vygotsky states that interaction is fundamental to development. It is not just a context for learning: it *is* learning. But to bring about change inter-action must stretch the learner: 'the only good learning is that which is in advance of development' (Vygotsky 1978:89).

The concept of situated cognition is also coherent with the *socio-cognitive* approach to construct definition implemented by Cambridge English, as presented in section 6.6.

1.2.2 Classroom concepts

The literature on learning-oriented assessment identifies a number of concepts which describe classroom interactions, identify conditions which favour learning, or distinguish the quality of learning. It is interesting to observe that they are increasingly understood in social constructivist terms (see section 3.3). Basic elements of classroom interaction include *tasks, goals, scaffolding, feedback* and *emergence.*

Tasks are activities designed to elicit learning interactions (see section 3.3.1). The concept of task plays an important part in the Learning Oriented Assessment model, as it is common to all of the 'four worlds' identified above. Thus it potentially provides a link between performance in the classroom, the social world, and in large-scale assessments. For Learning Oriented Assessment we define a learning task as one which leads to the *purposeful use of language to communicate personally significant meanings.*

Goals are what learners have in mind when engaging with a task. Several scholars have identified a distinction between *intrinsic* and *extrinsic* goals (using a variety of terms). Intrinsic goals focus on completing the task at hand – they are meaning focused – while extrinsic goals focus on other incentives, such as winning praise (so may be less effective for learning).

Scaffolding is the term frequently used to describe the support given to learners performing a task. In a social constructivist view scaffolding ensures that genuine task-focused interaction is enabled at a level of challenge which will lead to learning.

Feedback concerns the insight which the learner gains from engaging with a task (see section 3.3.3). There is extensive literature on the features of feedback which favour or disfavour learning. A social constructivist view sees feedback as akin to scaffolding, in that it describes the rapid sequence of turns (teacher–student or student–student) which constitute engagement with an interactive task.

Emergence concerns the process whereby a learner comes to speak a language. It captures the insight that communicative language ability is an outcome of learning which is qualitatively different from and at a higher level to conscious study of the inputs (see section 3.3.5).

1.3 What is language learning?

This section largely summarises Chapter 4.

The Learning Oriented Assessment model is essentially subject neutral, but this volume places a particular focus on languages. In education languages play several roles:

- as '*first*' languages
- as '*foreign*' languages
- as the *language of schooling.*

Any intervention in a particular context of language learning should recognise these several aspects of languages across and beyond the curriculum.

1.3.1 Second Language Acquisition studies

Learning Oriented Assessment for languages can also turn for insight to the branch of applied linguistics concerned with Second Language Acquisition (SLA).

*   The review of SLA included here is brief and selective, looking at models of learning relevant to the socio-cognitive approach adopted in this volume (see section 4.4). The key topics are listed below.

*   *Processing accounts* (see section 4.4.1) study why learners do not always pick up grammatical features present in oral or written input.

*   *Complexity theory* (see section 4.4.2) provides support for the idea that language is a *complex adaptive system* which emerges from the interactions of speakers communicating with one another, rather than the learning of rules. This is closer to the social constructivist view.

*   *Frequency-based accounts* (see section 4.4.3) inform approaches to introducing and sequencing learning material: more frequently encountered forms and collocations are likely to be learned before less frequently encountered ones.

*   *Complex Adaptive System Principles (CASP)* (see section 4.4.4) use empirical data to model how the need to communicate drives dual strategies: maximising communicative power while minimising cognitive effort. This demonstrates in compelling fashion the link between learning and satisfying the need to communicate, which is at the heart of the learning-oriented model.

1.4 What is to be learned?

This section summarises Chapter 5, and at its centre is formal education.

1.4.1 The desired outcomes of learning

Turning to our second question: in the case of language learning most would agree that the main objective should be to achieve a useful communicative competence in one or more languages. But in a social constructivist view that objective is best achieved and maintained through life as part of a transformation of the learner's dispositions, attitudes and practical learning skills. A very positive outcome of learning would thus be that students acquire the valuable dispositions and life skills that enable them to continue learning throughout life. Whether or not this *outcome* can or should be made an explicit curricular *objective* is an important question to address later.

1.4.2 Language proficiency: Construct definition

A second aspect to the question 'what is to be learned?' concerns how we define 'language proficiency' in order to test or teach it. We must define a specific *construct*: a theory or model of what knowing a language entails (see section 5.2).

1.4.3 The content of learning: Curricular objectives

Constructs relate to the communicative competences which are the desired *outcome* of learning. The third aspect to the question 'what is to be learned?' concerns curricular objectives: the *inputs* to learning (see section 5.3). Understanding how inputs relate to outputs requires us to address the important concept of *emergence*: communicative competence is a 'higher-order skill' qualitatively different to the conscious study of elements of content (see section 3.3.5). This will lead the Learning Oriented Assessment model to make a distinction between *learner-centred* and *curriculum-centred* views of classroom interaction.

1.5 The roles of assessment in learning

This section summarises Chapters 6 and 7, and at its centre are the complementary roles of large-scale and classroom assessment.

Classroom assessment and large-scale assessment play complementary roles in Learning Oriented Assessment, but share the same basic process: they are centred on tasks, which stimulate language activity, in conditions enabling observation, evaluation, feedback and learning.

These two dimensions of assessment produce different kinds of *evidence,* complementary to each other and contributing to the dual purposes of assessment: to provide evidence *for* learning and *of* learning.

1.5.1 Proficiency and achievement testing: Measurement and meaning

Learning Oriented Assessment's primary requirement of large-scale assessment is that it should test *proficiency*, that is, should be *criterion referenced* to uses of language in the real world. This involves firstly identifying where students are in their learning, on a path from beginner to advanced, and secondly describing what it means to be there (see section 6.1).

There is also a place in Learning Oriented Assessment for a simpler kind of interpretation: tests to measure *achievement* of curricular objectives may be useful and necessary.

The distinction between proficiency and achievement parallels that between treating language as a skill or as a body of knowledge – focusing on what learners can do, or on what they have learned. A main focus on proficiency testing should help teachers and students to keep sight of the higher-order objective – communicative language ability.

Large-scale assessment has to focus both on the quality of the measurement, termed *reliability*, as well as the quality of the interpretation, termed *validity* (see section 6.6).

Chapter 6 offers a non-technical introduction to the measurement of psychological traits: the notion of an ability scale (see section 6.2), the approach to measurement (see sections 6.3, 6.4), and the approach to performance testing for the skills of writing and speaking (see section 6.5).

1.5.2 Evidence *of* and *for* learning: Large-scale assessment

Large-scale assessment as presented in Chapter 6 has significant strengths. It focuses on proficiency, relating what is learned to ability in a 'real world'. It uses a strong measurement model ensuring comparable and interpretable measures. These should be crucial factors in defining how a school subject is conceived and taught, maintaining the focus on useful learning outcomes. Good summative assessment can thus provide evidence both of learning and for learning, complementary to evidence that can be collected in the classroom.

1.5.3 The nature of Learning Oriented Assessment in the classroom

This overview chapter has already introduced the essential elements of a learning-oriented approach to classroom interaction:

- the higher-order objective of communicative language ability is qualitatively different to lower-level curricular objectives, but both are important
- the transferable skills of learning how to learn are a key outcome
- using language purposefully will trigger language acquisition processes similar to those involved in learning a first language
- learning is more effective where learners are oriented towards engaging with the communicative task at hand, rather than on achieving a good mark
- effective scaffolding and feedback is an essential element of classroom interaction
- giving students an orientation as to their progress is valuable in enabling them to take control of their learning.

The learning-oriented classroom assigns specific responsibilities for learning to students and teachers. The onus is on students to develop the skills which will make them autonomous learners. Teachers may have several roles, including perhaps that of conducting formal assessment, but their central task is to create an environment in which the responsibility for learning is shared between students and teachers.

1.5.4 Evidence *of* and *for* learning: Learning-oriented classroom assessment

The evidence from classroom-based learning is used primarily by students and teachers, with the primary function of feeding back into further learning (see section 7.4).

Classroom work provides ongoing evidence of and for learning, complementary to external assessment. While the strength of large-scale assessment lies in the degree of control and standardisation of the conditions under which performances are elicited and evaluated, classroom performance is more complex to deal with, because such control and standardisation is neither possible nor desirable.

1.6 Aligning large-scale and classroom assessment

In the previous sections we looked at the roles of large-scale assessment and classroom assessment, and the complementary forms of evidence of and for learning which they may contribute. A final step is to align these within a comprehensive model of Learning Oriented Assessment, linking evidence from all levels into a coherent and co-ordinated system. Figures 1.4 and 1.5 attempt to portray such an aligned system (please note that Learning Oriented Assessment is abbreviated to LOA in the figures).

Figure 1.4 portrays a macro level, at which objectives are defined and outcomes monitored, and a micro level (the classroom), which is where learning actually happens. To focus first on the macro level: it provides a frame of reference – the CEFR, in this illustration – which locates objectives and outcomes in a real world of language use. From this, high-level objectives and specific lower-level content are developed, producing a Learning Oriented Assessment syllabus. An external exam helps define learning goals and is one source of evidence for evaluating outcomes.

The structured record of achievement accepts evidence from a range of sources, including the external exam, and is interpretable in terms of the frame of reference – that is, the higher-level goals of learning. However, Figure 1.5 indicates that the record can also serve a summative monitoring purpose, to the extent that monitoring the achievement of specific curriculum objectives is deemed to be important.

Figure 1.5 expands the micro level to illustrate the basic Learning Oriented

Figure 1.4 Evidence for learning: The macro level

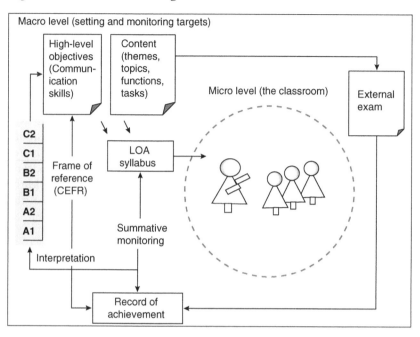

Figure 1.5 Evidence for learning: The micro level

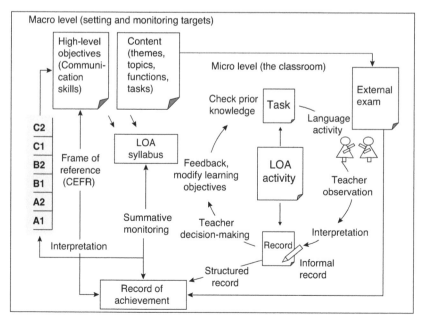

Assessment cycle of classroom activity: engagement with a task, producing observable performance, which is interpreted, possibly providing various kinds of informal record; evaluation leads to feedback and modification or continuation of the lesson plan.

Alignment of the different sources of evidence is the subject of Chapter 8.

1.7 In summary

This overview chapter has presented Learning Oriented Assessment as a system which brings together complementary evidence from classroom activity and from large-scale assessment to achieve the twin goals of better measurement and better learning outcomes. It adopts a particular model of learning – social constructivism – which is coherent with how language learning is currently understood, for example, in the action-oriented model of the CEFR, and a socio-cognitive, construct-based approach to assessment, as exemplified in the approach developed by Cambridge English.

It asserts that a valuable outcome of successful learning is that students acquire the dispositions, attitudes and skills that constitute learning how to learn: life skills which many believe are transferable across disciplines, to the extent that learning is understood as a process of personal development.

The key role of interaction in learning suggests a task-based approach to developing higher-order communicative skills, and also makes clear that these skills are qualitatively different to and more than the simple sum of lower-level curricular objectives.

Large-scale proficiency testing can provide valuable evidence of learning, focusing on the important outcomes and providing an orientation to learners and teachers. Classroom learning-oriented interaction is where learning actually happens, and provides complementary evidence to feed back into further learning.

Finally, all sources of evidence are aligned to the same higher-order objectives and a common understanding of standards, ensuring system-wide coherence, and outcomes which all partners in the educational process can understand and share.

2 The roots of Learning Oriented Assessment

'The value of any fact or theory as bearing on human activity is, in the long run, determined by practical application – that is by using it for accomplishing some definite purpose.'

What Psychology Can Do for the Teacher (John Dewey and Alexander McLellan 1908:195)

This chapter reviews the different contexts in which learning-oriented approaches have been developed, and explains why this aspect of assessment should be emphasised in the practice of examination providers such as Cambridge English.

Learning-oriented assessment is one of several terms used in recent years to identify a similar concern: to promote better learning. Whatever the term used – classroom-based assessment, assessment for learning, learning-oriented assessment, or others referred to below – these movements start by challenging the priorities and values of educational assessment as currently understood and practised. Learning-oriented approaches 'signify a more teacher-mediated, context-based, classroom embedded assessment practice', and are 'explicitly or implicitly defined in opposition to traditional externally set and assessed large scale formal examinations' (Davison and Leung 2009:395).

Naturally, a large number of different terms have been used in naming or describing these movements. Turner (2012) asks whether an 'umbrella term' is needed to unite the concepts underlying this range of labels. In fact, these movements differ according to their precise motivation, reflecting the context in which they arose. We are not looking at a single, coherent movement, even if much of the foundational literature on the subject has been widely shared. A review of some of the different contexts will show the common ground, while providing a more nuanced picture.

Concerning terminology: as Turner points out, terms have been used with different meanings by different writers. In this text we will attempt to be consistent in our use of terms. Assessments of the kind provided by Cambridge English will be called *large-scale assessment*, following Pellegrino, Chudowsky and Glaser (2001), rather than *standardised*, *external*, *high-stakes*, *summative* or other adjectives that we might also have chosen. Reference in general terms to approaches which prioritise learning will use the adjective *learning-oriented*, in lower case; but where specific movements have adopted different terminology we will use that. The Cambridge systemic model presented in this volume is referred to as Learning Oriented Assessment, capitalised.

2.1 Cambridge English and Learning Oriented Assessment

The Cambridge English approach to Learning Oriented Assessment is a response to significant developments in the way that Cambridge exams are used, and in the profile of test takers. Traditionally candidates came from private language schools: willing, self-motivated students, studying in classes of similar ability, at an appropriate level. These were ideal conditions for learning. The situation is changing as the Cambridge English exams are increasingly adopted at state or institutional level for use in primary or secondary education. These entail more diverse circumstances for learning, presenting new opportunities, but also new issues, challenges and responsibilities – above all, to ensure that the impact of the intervention is a positive one. Learning Oriented Assessment may be understood as the theory of action which addresses this challenge.

2.2 Origins and emphases of learning-oriented approaches

In the sections below we describe some specific contexts which motivated the development of particular learning-oriented movements or methods. Where possible we have located these in a specific country or region, but this does not of course mean that similar motivations were not at work elsewhere.

2.2.1 Assessment for Learning: England

The terms Assessment for Learning, or formative assessment, are now chiefly associated with the work of the Assessment Reform Group (ARG), a collaboration of academics largely from the University of Cambridge and King's College London, School of Education, which was formed in 1989 and disbanded itself in 2010. They did not invent the term 'formative assessment', which was first used with its current meaning by Bloom (1969), but their development of the concept has proved influential worldwide. A report of the farewell event offers a retrospective summary of their work and its impact (Mansell 2010). The ARG started life as a task force analysing the likely impact on assessment of the 1988 Education Reform Act, which envisaged a far-reaching reorganisation of state schooling, including the instigation of a national assessment system.

The ARG's first review of existing research on assessment identified what their later work would confirm:

- the problems caused by using assessment results to evaluate schools, rather than individual pupils

- a consequent recognition of the need to separate formative from summative purposes of assessment
- an implied need for greater trust in teachers (Assessment Reform Group 1992).

These issues determined the direction of the group's later work.

The group's focus on using assessment to support learning became a major research project, which resulted in Black and Wiliam's (1998a) paper 'Assessment and Classroom Learning'. A book followed: *Inside the Black Box* (Black and Wiliam 1998b) which attracted worldwide interest, providing as it did apparently compelling evidence, based on synthesised results from 250 assessment-related studies, that formative assessment could significantly improve schools' performance.

The ARG's case for formative assessment was sufficiently compelling to secure its endorsement by the UK Qualifications and Curriculum Authority, who had a poster outlining 10 principles of assessment for learning sent to every school in England (see Appendix 1).

Further areas of research undertaken by members of the ARG included systematic reviews of the impact on students of self- and peer-assessment (Sebba and Deakin Crick 2005); the reliability and validity of assessment by teachers for summative purposes (Harlen 2004); the impact of summative assessment and tests on students' motivation for learning (Harlen and Deakin Crick 2002).

The group's last major publication before they disbanded (Mansell, James and the Assessment Reform Group 2009), jointly published with the Teaching and Learning Research Programme (TLRP), offers a final summary assessment of what the group considered to have been achieved, and a critique of the state of educational assessment in the UK. The test-heavy situation in England is compared unfavourably with that in Scotland, where national assessment of all pupils had been abandoned 'because policy-makers recognised that teachers were teaching to the tests and that, although it appeared that results were improving, it was more likely to be that teachers were getting better at rehearsing children for the tests' (Mansell et al 2009:6).

The group acknowledges the difficulty of successfully implementing assessment for learning; it challenges teachers to change what they do, how they think about learning and teaching, and the way in which they relate to their pupils. The case for involving teachers in summative assessment is endorsed.

The importance of aligning assessment and learning is stressed (illustrated in the example of school mathematics), and the consequent need for clear construct definition – what is the purpose of the subject, and how can this purpose be made the object of measurement?

The paper is addressed to policy-makers, and lists four pressing challenges for them:

- Putting effective in-class assessment into practice system wide: the 'spirit' of assessment for learning is hard to achieve. Relatively few teachers use assessment for learning techniques effectively to promote learner autonomy.
- Enhancing confidence in tests and examinations: data from tests and examinations has been re-purposed to negative effect: 'there is little doubt that policies such as performance tables, targets and Ofsted inspections that place great weight on test and examination data have driven behaviour in schools' (Mansell et al 2009:24).
- Justifying the costs of assessment: 'Extraordinary sums of money are now devoted to our assessment systems in the UK. The key question is whether these resources could be better spent' (Mansell et al 2009:17).
- Avoiding micro-management: abandoning scholarly distance, the authors vent their frustration at the government in England, which:

> has developed a version of assessment for learning which shares little of the "spirit" of the definition and principles from the Assessment Reform Group, although the documentation quotes them. Indeed, *Assessing Pupils' Progress*, the in-class assessment system that is a part of the government's version of assessment for learning in England, is more to do with specifying frequent summative assessment than formative assessment (Mansell et al 2009:20).

The ARG's critical appraisal of the state of assessment in England can thus be summarised as follows: its impact on individuals and schools makes assessment a high-stakes event. The consequent focus on achieving good grades negatively impacts intrinsic interest in the subject. Harlen (2005:207) points to the vast amount of accumulated evidence of the 'detrimental effects' that repeated external testing can do to students, teaching and the curriculum.

Reliability is interpreted in norm-referenced terms, ranking students against each other, rather than against clearly identified learning goals, thus decreasing the relevance and value of what is actually measured.

Therefore the *validity* of such assessment – whether it actually serves the educational objectives that we would wish it to – can be challenged: 'we use what are a very blunt set of instruments to intervene in the highly sensitive and complex business of learning' (Broadfoot 2005:127). In this view validity would be better achieved by engaging teachers more directly in summative assessment.

But all of these issues can be brought back to a single underlying cause: the re-purposing of assessments designed to accredit students' achievement to serve as instruments of *accountability*, providing evidence to judge the performance of schools. This puts pressure on teachers to teach to the tests, leading to a negative impact on classroom practice and on learning. As Mansell et al (2009:7) describe the situation in England: 'Assessment information has become a proxy measure that is supposed to facilitate judgments on the quality of most elements of our education system: its teachers, head teachers, schools, support services, local authorities and even the government itself.'

The government is accused of using assessment inappropriately as a managerial tool to raise standards by creating competition between individuals, teachers and schools, commodifying the curriculum (making it measurable through standards), and using outcomes to reward or punish performance. Such use of performance indicators inevitably backfires.

We should note that the ARG's critical appraisal of the role of large-scale assessment is aimed primarily at government policy in England, and the managerial model of using assessment as a lever within education, in contrast for example with developments in Scotland.

Some of the ARG's research was undertaken within the TLRP, which ran from 1999 to 2012. Now an archive, the TLRP website (Teaching and Learning Research Programme 2013) provides a detailed account of the wide range of activities and studies undertaken within the TLRP. The programme was concerned to maximise its impact on educational policy. While the huge body of research undertaken cannot be synthesised here, the TLRP's own synthesis, in the form of 10 'evidence-informed principles for teaching and learning or pedagogies', might be seen to offer an evidence-based definition of learning-oriented assessment. These principles are included in Appendix 2.

2.2.2 Flight from psychometric testing: The United States

In the United States as in England there was a reaction against accountability testing; and in particular many calls for reform reflected disenchantment with psychometric testing (e.g. the predominant use of multiple-choice items). The terms *alternative* and *authentic* assessment seem to co-occur, indicating a concern that learning required different approaches to assessment, and that testing should somehow involve 'real-life' tasks.

Authentic measures are: 'engaging and worthy problems or questions of importance, in which students must use knowledge to fashion performances effectively and creatively. The tasks are either replicas of or analogous to the kinds of problems faced by adult citizens and consumers or professionals in the field' (Wiggins 1993:229).

Linn, Baker and Dunbar (1991) identify a shift in assessment policy and practice aiming at *direct assessment* of complex performances, using open-ended problems, essays, hands-on science problems and portfolios.

> Collectively such measures are frequently referred to as "authentic" assessments . . . because they involve the performance of tasks that are valued in their own right. In contrast, paper-and-pencil, multiple-choice tests derive their value primarily as *indicators* or *correlates* of other valued performances (Linn et al 1991:3, emphasis added).

Linn et al identify the lack of correspondence between learning goals and indicators of achievement as an increasingly important concern for traditional tests of achievement, and a substantial motivation behind pleas for 'authentic' assessment.

Wiggins' (1998:12) concept of 'Educative Assessment' argues for 'testing that is deliberately designed to teach and improve, not just measure'. Wiggins and McTighe (1998:15) offer a 'backwards design' model for using assessment to drive curriculum and learning, providing a detailed 'process and set of tools . . . to make the selection of curriculum priorities more likely to happen by design than by good fortune'.

Brown and Hudson (1998) consider the impact of external assessments in terms of *washback* – the negative or positive effect on classroom practice. They particularly associate negative washback with standardised testing (i.e. multiple choice, item based), recognising that well-designed performance assessments can provide strong positive washback.

Brown and Hudson list a range of *alternative assessment* procedures: checklists, journals, logs, videotapes and audiotapes, self-evaluation, teacher observations, portfolios, conferences, diaries, self-assessments, and peer-assessments. Their review is positive but critical, challenging the wilder claims made for such approaches, e.g. by Huerta-Macías (1995:10), who argues that 'alternative assessments are in and of themselves valid, due to the direct nature of the assessment'. Brown and Hudson point out that the use of authentic materials does not absolve testers from the requirement to justify how information is collected and interpreted (the same point is made by Bennett (2011, see also section 8.4).

The aim to measure competence through authentic tasks leads naturally to the adoption of criterion-referenced *standards* as a basis for evaluating school achievements. In the United States context Hudson (2012) dates to the late 1970s 'a long history of concern with *standards-based* instruction', portraying it as a reaction to poor performance in international educational measures of science and mathematics. The standards movement thus emerged in the reaction against the dominance of psychometric tests. Hudson introduces the concepts of *content* and *performance* standards: what students should know, and what level of performance on skills they should be able to demonstrate.

Shepard (2000:8–9) is critical of the evolution of the standards-based movement in the US, which 'has . . . placed great faith in externally imposed standards and "tests worth teaching to." More recently, the standards movement has been corrupted, in many instances, into a heavy-handed system of rewards and punishments without the capacity building and professional development originally proposed as part of the vision.' Shepard here is criticising the same managerial use of assessment to 'drive up standards' as that which was identified on the other side of the Atlantic by the ARG.

2.2.3 Teachers at the centre: Australia, New Zealand, Hong Kong, Scotland

Davison and Leung (2009) and Davison (2007) use the terms *teacher-based* and *school-based assessment* (TBA and SBA) to describe some major assessment reform programmes (see section 4.1). These developments give teachers an important role in assessing learning objectives which could not be easily assessed in public examinations, while at the same time aiming to enhance teaching and learning. They denote a shift from traditional norm-referenced external examinations towards a more student-centred TBA approach. Such projects substantially re-define the role of teachers entailing among other things a considerable training requirement.

Carless (2007), reporting on a project in Hong Kong, claims to be the first to use the term learning-oriented assessment, though there are other contenders. As he explains, he coined the term in an attempt to emphasise the learning features of assessment and promote their development, but also to distance it from the term 'formative' which through its various forms of interpretation in Hong Kong had acquired negative connotations among teachers. He proposes three principles of learning-oriented assessment:

1. Assessment tasks should be designed to stimulate sound learning practices amongst students.
2. Assessment should involve students actively in engaging with criteria, quality, their own and/or peers' performance.
3. Feedback should be timely and forward looking so as to support current and future student learning.

Davison and Leung (2009) present TBA as policy-supported practice in a number of educational systems internationally, including:

- Australia, for example in Queensland, where SBA was introduced in the 1970s. Here TBA is used for all assessment in the secondary school, even for high-stakes purposes (Queensland Studies Authority 2009), although not without problems with the quality and the norm-referencing of school-based assessments (Withers 1987).
- New Zealand, which also has a long history of SBA in the senior secondary school New Zealand Qualifications Authority (no date).
- Canada (Cumming and Maxwell 2004).

- Scotland (Learning and Teaching Scotland 2006).
- TBA is increasingly being adopted as national educational policy in Asia: in Hong Kong (Carless 2008, 2009, Davison 2007, Davison and Hamp-Lyons 2009), Singapore (Cheah 1998), as well as in some developing countries.

Davison and Leung observe that it is also promoted in the United States (Popham 2008, Stiggins 2008), although, as they note, 'always over-shadowed by national testing programs' (2009:394). The requirement to professionalise teachers' role in assessment is addressed, for example, by Brindley (2001), who uses the term *outcomes-based assessment* in relation to focusing teachers' judgements on performance criteria, and proposes practical technical and professional approaches to achieving this.

2.2.4 Re-thinking assessment's role in society

Shepard (2000) identifies the need for a paradigm shift in conceptions of assessment. 'The best way to understand dissonant current practices . . . is to realize that instruction (at least in its ideal form) is drawn from the emergent paradigm while testing is held over from the past' (Shepard 2000:4).

Shepard criticises current approaches to assessment as reflecting outworn beliefs about education in society, cognition, and the nature of learning.

> The central ideas of social efficiency and scientific management . . . were closely linked, respectively, to hereditarian theories of individual differences and to associationist and behaviorist learning theories. These psychological theories were, in turn, served by scientific measurement of ability and achievement (2000:4).

Shepard uses the term classroom-based assessment (CBA) to advance a social constructivist conceptual framework, stressing that 'a singularly important idea in this new paradigm is that both development and learning are primarily social processes' (2000:7).

Thus, the view of education as an obstacle course which relatively few participants successfully negotiate may have served society well enough in the past, but is now at odds with the needs of a learning society and a knowledge economy, which seek the best possible outcome for every student.

This is of course an ethical as much as an economic issue. Lynch's discussion of alternative assessment extends conceptions of assessment to include a wider range of activities, which have in common 'the systematic use of information for making decisions and judgments about individuals' (Lynch 2001:359). Lynch interprets critical theory to acknowledge 'a concern for changing the human and social world, not just describing it, i.e., the "transformative agenda", with the related and motivational concern for social justice and equality' (2001:357). He describes work to create a validity framework which 'integrates validity with ethical considerations, especially in terms of consciously addressing the power relations that are at play in the assessment context'. Lynch links this ethical concern to Bachman and Palmer's (1996) test 'usefulness' framework, and also to Messick's (1989) 'consequential validity': the concern with the value implications and social consequences of test interpretation and use (see section 6.6). Such concerns have been echoed by others in the critical language testing school of thought (e.g. Shohamy 1997).

Rethinking the role of assessment also requires us to recognise that in today's world learning is a continuous lifelong process. *Sustainable assessment* (Boud 2000, Boud and Falchikov 2006, see also section 3.4.1) relates to the context of higher education, which must 'equip students to learn beyond the academy once the infrastructure of teachers, courses and formal assessment is no longer available' (Boud and Falchikov 2006:399). Such skills concern the ability to learn continuously through participating in social activity, particularly the workplace.

Language skills in particular have important uses in professional contexts. *Performance assessment* is the term used by McNamara (1996) in relation to the development of a language assessment for medical professionals. McNamara stresses the complexity of dealing with the communicative skills entailed by such a programme, referring to it as 'opening Pandora's box' (1996:48).

2.2.5 Assessment as a strong model of learning

There are several assessment techniques which set out to produce better learning through the adoption of quite specific theoretical or process models.

Dynamic assessment (Anton 2012, Lantolf and Poehner 2011) implements a specific form of teacher–student interaction exploiting Vygotsky's (1986) notion of the *zone of proximal development*. *Cognitive acceleration* (see section 2.4.3) is a procedure which focuses in the same way on specific forms of learning interaction. A third somewhat similar concept is that of *mastery learning* (Whiting, Van Burg and Render 1995) (see section 2.4.1), which involves regular testing and feedback to students, who either achieve a high test score and proceed to the next task, or continue to study the topic further until they can satisfy the mastery criterion.

Black and Wiliam (2009:23, see also section 2.3) describe these approaches as formative assessment based on particularly effective versions of classroom interactive dialogue.

Wiggins' (1998) above-mentioned concept of 'Educative Assessment' also qualifies in this category.

Learning Oriented Assessment as developed in this volume also aspires to fit into this category. First presented by Jones, Saville and Hamilton (2013) it sets out to define an integrated, ecological system, offering complementary roles for assessment and teaching expertise, and based on a specific model of learning.

2.3 Defining learning-oriented assessment: Process, policy or principles?

This volume sets out to define a model of Learning Oriented Assessment in terms of principles – that is, of theory – in line with Bennett (2011), who insists that assessment for learning must be defined in terms of an explicit theory of action.

This section looks critically at how learning-oriented approaches have been described and presented: as statements of policy, theoretically motivated principles, educational values, outcomes-oriented recommendations for action, characteristic features, or perhaps a mixture of all these. We will focus on the ARG's definitions of formative assessment, or assessment for learning, chiefly because this group defined and re-defined the concept over an extended period. We would wish to identify the essential features, because a useful theory of learning-oriented assessment will be specific and limited in scope. The exercise will also enable a condensed review of many of the definitions, descriptions and features of learning-oriented assessment proposed by some key actors over time.

The ARG's writings reflect an awareness of the dual need to develop a theory of formative assessment, as well as to devise practical prescriptions that teachers could make sense of. Their successive articulations of formative assessment, or assessment for learning, developed and changed over time. One of their early statements is quoted below. Written for dissemination within the educational community, it takes a largely process-oriented approach to defining formative assessment, based on the work of Black and Wiliam (1998a).

This research indicated that improving learning through assessment depends on five, deceptively simple, key factors:

- the provision of effective feedback to pupils;
- the active involvement of pupils in their own learning;
- adjusting teaching to take account of the results of assessment;
- a recognition of the profound influence assessment has on the motivation and self-esteem of pupils, both of which are crucial influences on learning;
- the need for pupils to be able to assess themselves and understand how to improve (Assessment Reform Group 1999:4).

These positive principles are followed by several 'inhibiting factors', including:

- a tendency for teachers to assess quantity of work and presentation rather than the quality of learning;
- greater attention given to marking and grading, much of it tending to lower the self-esteem of pupils, rather than to providing advice for improvement;
- a strong emphasis on comparing pupils with each other which demoralises the less successful learners;
- teachers' feedback to pupils often serves social and managerial purposes rather than helping them to learn more effectively;
- teachers not knowing enough about their pupils' learning needs (Assessment Reform Group 1999:5).

These latter statements are process-oriented descriptions of how *not* to behave. Taken as a whole, this early statement provides a set of concrete prescriptions for how classroom practice should proceed, albeit at quite a high level of abstraction.

A later ARG document (Assessment Reform Group 2002, the poster put up in every school in England) provides the following list of headings, which are each glossed in more detail (Appendix 1 has the complete text).

Assessment for learning:

1. is part of effective planning
2. focuses on how students learn
3. is central to classroom practice
4. is a key professional skill
5. has an emotional impact
6. affects learner motivation
7. promotes commitment to learning goals and assessment criteria
8. helps learners know how to improve
9. encourages self-assessment
10. recognises all achievements.

The above headings offer a very different description or definition of what constitutes assessment for learning: a more comprehensive range of characteristics and suggested impacts, but at a level of greater generality. As the document explains: 'the principles have been drafted and redrafted many times and have benefited from comments from a number of individuals and associations, whose help is gratefully acknowledged.' Perhaps this explains the more wide-ranging and inclusive, but less focused, approach to description.

The poster also includes ARG's most often-quoted definition of Assessment for Learning:

> Assessment for Learning is the process of seeking and interpreting evidence for use by learners and their teachers to decide where the learners are in their learning, where they need to go and how best to get there (Assessment Reform Group 2002).

In contrast, Black and Wiliam focus increasingly narrowly over time on a search for the essence of formative assessment. Eleven years after the foundational paper (Black and Wiliam 1998a) which provided the major impetus for Assessment for Learning, Black and Wiliam (2009) track their own progress from describing formative assessment as a series of processes, to reconceptualising it as a set of principles:

> Early work on formative assessment centred on five main types of activity, suggested by evidence of their potential effectiveness:
> 1. Sharing success criteria with learners
> 2. Classroom questioning
> 3. Comment-only marking
> 4. Peer- and self-assessment
> 5. Formative use of summative tests (Black and Wiliam 2009:3).

They acknowledge the lack of a theoretical foundation for this list of activities. In search of a better theoretical grounding for formative assessment, they draw on Ramaprasad's (1983) three key processes in learning and teaching:

1. Establishing where the learners are in their learning.
2. Establishing where they are going.
3. Establishing what needs to be done to get them there.

(Note that this is the source of the 'iconic' definition of Assessment for Learning quoted above.) Observing that these indicate roles for both teachers and students led Black and Wiliam to identify the following five aspects of formative assessment:

> 1. Clarifying and sharing learning intentions and criteria for success;
> 2. Engineering effective classroom discussions and other learning tasks that elicit evidence of student understanding;
> 3. Providing feedback that moves learners forward;
> 4. Activating students as instructional resources for one another; and
> 5. Activating students as the owners of their own learning (2009:4).

They link these back to the five types of activity identified earlier, which they now see as ways of *enacting* these five key strategies. For example, classroom questioning is merely one way of implementing strategy 2, and comment-only marking is a particular way that teachers might achieve strategy 3.

Black and Wiliam re-state their definition of formative assessment, drawing both on their earlier definitions (Black and Wiliam 1998a) and the definition of ARG (Assessment Reform Group 2002):

Practice in a classroom is formative to the extent that evidence about student achievement is elicited, interpreted, and used by teachers, learners, or their peers, to make decisions about the next steps in instruction that are likely to be better, or better founded, than the decisions they would have taken in the absence of the evidence that was elicited.

A discussion of this carefully worded definition makes clear that formative assessment is concerned with 'the creation of, and capitalization upon, "moments of contingency" in instruction for the purpose of the regulation of learning processes' (Assessment Reform Group 2002).

This, they acknowledge, seems to be a very narrow focus, but one which helps to distinguish a theory of formative assessment from an overall theory of teaching and learning. They insist that, although narrow, the concept has far-reaching implications for instructional design, curriculum, pedagogy, psychology and epistemology (Black and Wiliam 1998a:8).

This explicit narrowing of focus is reflected and justified in Black and Wiliam's acknowledgement that the five earlier listed aspects of formative assessment reflect 'very general principles of learning, notably social constructivism and meta-cognition' (2009:19). In contrast they present with approval two distinctive programmes of instruction – cognitive acceleration (see section 2.4.3) and dynamic assessment (see section 2.4.2) – which prioritise the improvement of learning capacity over subject-specific aims, using an explicit and detailed theory of learning. Characteristic of both programmes is their explicit theoretical basis, the definition of a specified set of classroom activities, and prescribed pedagogic practices for which teachers require specific training. Black and Wiliam report that these approaches are found to lead to significant long-term improvements in school achievement, and that the improvements they secure extend beyond the particular subject context in which a programme has been implemented.

Describing these approaches as formative assessment based on particularly effective versions of classroom interactive dialogue, they acknowledge that in comparison with cognitive acceleration and dynamic assessment programmes, 'any teacher using formative and interactive dialogue . . . for normal subject teaching is engaged in a more diffuse and subject-specific form of thinking skills programme' (Black and Wiliam 2009:23).

To the extent that the practice of standard classroom teaching is necessarily 'diffuse and subject specific' the aspiration to construct a theory of formative assessment distinct from an overall theory of teaching and learning seems attractive.

We will follow Black and Wiliam in seeking to define Learning Oriented Assessment as narrowly as possible, and, indeed, their location of the essence of formative assessment in the dialogic interaction between teacher and student is close to the position which will be developed here (see Chapter 8).

This section has focused on treatments of formative assessment associated with ARG's work in England; but of course other writers have provided similar, more or less discursive descriptions or definitions of learning-oriented assessment. For example, the TLRP offered a synthesis of its findings in the form of 10 'evidence-informed principles' of effective pedagogy (Teaching and Learning Research Programme 2007), the full text of which is provided in Appendix 2.

2.4 Specific learning-oriented methods

2.4.1 Mastery learning

Black and Wiliam (1998a) provide an account of mastery learning as a practical implementation of the learning theories of John B Carroll. They describe two main approaches to mastery learning developed in the 1960s: one by Benjamin Bloom, using teacher-paced group-based teaching approaches, called Learning for Mastery (LFM), and one by Keller, called a Personalized System of Instruction (PSI). The essence of the approach is that students continue to study a particular topic until they master it, however long this takes, before they are permitted to move on to the next topic. Black and Wiliam call mastery learning 'learning with a key formative element' and report research which found large positive effects (Kulik and Kulik 1989). However, they note that others have questioned whether mastery learning is effective at all. Slavin (1987) concluded from the reported studies that almost all of the large effect sizes were found on teacher-prepared, rather than standardised, tests: in other words, the effects were produced, consciously or unconsciously, by teaching to the test.

2.4.2 Dynamic assessment

Anton (2012) attributes the concept of dynamic assessment to Vygotsky, who referred to a change from *symptomatic assessment,* which focuses on present behaviour of a particular developmental stage, to *diagnostic assessment*, which focuses on future behaviour and on developing recommendations to foster developments. Two approaches to dynamic assessment are identified:

- interventionist, which follows a test–intervention–retest format and focuses on quantitative results
- interactionist, which attempts qualitative analysis and interpretation of the key features of the interaction, blending learning and assessment.

The latter is more in line with Vygotsky's original conception. Poehner (2008) insists that it is impossible to understand the full range of the learners' potential if mediation is detached from its dialogic context and if learners' contributions to the mediation are not interpreted within the whole interaction.

Poehner and Lantolf (2005) claim that a fundamental difference between dynamic assessment and formative assessment is that while the latter focuses on the completion of the task, dynamic assessment aims at cognitive development and transfer of skills to future tasks through intentional and systematic mediation. Thus it targets higher-order learning skills.

2.4.3 Cognitive acceleration

Cognitive acceleration (CA) is a technique which aims to promote cognitive development by stimulating cognitive processes according to a specific theoretical model. CA programmes were instituted in the early 1980s in London, targeting children aged 12–14 with a cognitive intervention set in a science context, called Cognitive Acceleration through Science Education (CASE), designed to promote the type of higher level thinking described by Inhelder and Piaget (1958) as 'formal operations'. Adey, Robertson and Venville (2002) report a study of children aged 5 or 6 years, aimed at the development of the level characterised as concrete operational thinking by Piaget and Inhelder. According to Adey et al's account of this study, specific theoretical principles underlying CA work include:

- *Cognitive conflict.* Starting with Piagetian notions of equilibration being attained at a higher level of thinking when a child encounters a problem which cannot be solved with existing cognitive structures, a graded challenge is offered to the target population of learners.
- *Social construction.* This draws on the Vygotskian notion that the construction of knowledge and understanding is a social process (see section 3.1), by designing appropriate group interactions into the interventions.
- *Metacognition.* In CA work this term means conscious reflection by a child on their own thinking processes, after a thinking act when they think back to the steps taken, and become aware how their own conceptualisation changed during the activity.
- *Schema theory.* The CA work in secondary school uses the schemata of formal operations described by Inhelder and Piaget (1958), while the study on 5- and 6-years-olds used the schema of concrete operational thinking.

The intervention consisted of a series of activities designed to provide cognitive conflict to 5-and 6-year-olds, to be delivered in a way which maximised opportunities for social construction, including metacognition. Significant positive effects of CA interventions have been reported.

3 What is learning?

'Education is a social process; education is growth; education is not preparation for life but is life itself.'

(John Dewey 1897)

Based on a broad review of the literature on learning and on formative assessment, this chapter introduces constructivism, and social constructivism in particular, as the learning paradigm within which our model of Learning Oriented Assessment can best be developed. We look at the building blocks of learning-oriented classroom interactions: tasks, scaffolding, and feedback, and at the roles of students and teachers.

3.1 Constructivism

In the preface to Jonassen and Land (Eds) (2012:iv) the authors identify the 1990s as the decade that 'has witnessed the most substantive and revolutionary changes in learning theory in history . . . Contemporary situated, sociocultural, and constructivist conceptions of learning are built on different ontological and epistemological foundations than communications theory, behaviorism, and cognitivism. We have entered a new age in learning theory.'

Sjøberg (2007:1) recounts the development of constructivism within education. The concept of *cognitive constructivism*, associated with Jean Piaget (Piaget 1976), proposes that learners cannot simply be given information which they immediately understand and use, but rather must construct their own knowledge. Experience enables them to create schemas – mental models of the world which are subsequently enlarged and refined through processes of assimilation and accommodation. Sjøberg points out that Piaget's own perspective was mostly on general aspects of the development of knowledge: 'He was not so much interested in education, let alone teaching or conditions for good and effective learning' (2007:7). Constructivism in education has latterly drawn on other theorists who put more stress on social and cultural conditions for learning. This concept of *social constructivism* is associated with Lev Vygotsky (Vygotsky 1986), who stresses the social and collaborative nature of learning. His most well-known construct is the *zone of proximal development*, which denotes the range of what a learner is currently able to assimilate, initially with the assistance of a more knowing interlocutor, such as a teacher. Vygotsky's concept makes an important distinction between learning and development:

> Learning which is oriented toward developmental levels that have already been reached is ineffective from the viewpoint of a child's overall development. It does not aim for a new stage of the developmental process, but rather lags behind this process. The only good learning is that which is in advance of development (Vygotsky 1978:82, in Black and Wiliam 2009:20).

Thus the zone of proximal development describes not just what a student can do with support, which might be simply learning, but also the maturing of new psychological functions. A focus in instruction on the maturing psychological functions is most likely to produce a transition to the next developmental level.

3.1.1 Constructivism and situated cognition

The two constructivist positions – cognitive and social – are by no means in conflict, but can be seen as different emphases within a general overarching concept of *situated cognition*: on an individual's cognition, or on the larger physical and social context of interactions and culturally constructed tools and meanings within which cognition develops.

Wilson and Myers (2000) give an account of *situated cognition theory*, asserting its potential to integrate the individual and the social within a coherent theoretical perspective:

> The stand-out characteristic of situated cognition seems to be the placement of individual cognition within the larger physical and social context of interactions and culturally constructed tools and meanings (Wilson and Myers 2000:66).

This characterisation resonates strongly with the socio-cognitive model at the heart of the CEFR and the approach to construct definition implemented by Cambridge English (see section 5.2).

Of course, locating the development of cognition in its social context adds complexity to attempts at description. How can the social context be adequately described or taken account of? Bronfenbrenner's (1979) *ecological systems theory* represents the learner's wider environment as a *complex dynamic system*, with interactions over five levels: a complex web linking the individual to the larger social structures of community, society, economics and politics. Ecological systems theory has had a far-reaching influence on the way that psychologists and social scientists approach the study of human beings and their environments. It is also important in the model of test impact developed by Saville (2009) which we return to in Chapter 9.

3.2 An appropriate model of cognition and learning

The social constructivist model of learning which we have placed at the centre of learning-oriented assessment seems particularly appropriate to language learning. We have illustrated its coherence with the action-oriented model of language learning proposed by the CEFR (see also section 5.1.1), and consequently with the Cambridge English approach to language assessment presented in Chapter 6.

Cambridge English Language Assessment is of course not alone among assessment providers in seeking ways to redefine the relationship between educational assessment and the process of learning and teaching; but in arriving at the systemic, ecological conception presented here, and in developing our model of cognition and learning, we have made choices which distinguish our approach from that of other assessment bodies.

One well-documented programme of work in the US looks to implement far more detailed models of competence, supported by even more powerful statistical methods. This programme goes back as far as Frederiksen, Mislevy and Bejar (Eds) (1993:19) who found that 'the view of human abilities implicit in standard test theory – Item Response Theory as well as classical true-score theory – is incompatible with the view rapidly emerging from cognitive and educational psychology'. In this view, trait-based measures fail to capture the complexity of abilities in the way necessary to understand learning or impact positively on it. Data to inform learning must be collected using detailed cognitive models, and approaches to measurement that can deal with them. This programme has been pursued through two major projects at the Educational Testing Service (ETS): work on evidence-centred design (ECD) (Mislevy, Steinberg and Almond 1999), and on cognitive diagnosis approaches (CDA) (Xu and von Davier 2006). The focus on cognition has clear relevance to formative assessment, and is developed in this direction by Pellegrino et al (2001).

However, the cognitive approach as presented by Pellegrino et al is illustrated chiefly by examples from maths and science, where the stress is more on metacognitive problem-solving. With its focus on the individual's cognition it lacks the social constructivist insight that 'both development and learning are primarily social processes' (Shepard 2000:7). Thus it appears to focus more narrowly on the attainment of curricular objectives and understanding of concepts, and to have less relevance to the nature of formative classroom interaction, or to the skills, dispositions and attitudes that inspire further learning (James and Brown 2005:10–11).

The approach proposed by Pellegrino et al (2001) prompts some questions. Firstly, diagnosis is only a starting point for formative activity, which, as we have insisted, entails *interaction*; and thus a pivotal role for teachers, as participants in or co-ordinators of that interaction.

Secondly, when we consider the nature of formative interactions within the classroom it becomes clear that learners' states of understanding or mastery can hardly be analysed in isolation from the interactions themselves (Teasdale and Leung 2000). Cognition is socially constructed and begins in interaction. Model-based diagnosis of cognitive attributes requires stable observations, something hardly to be expected at the growing point where learning is happening. It is easier to see the relevance to summative than to formative assessment (Jones 2012:360).

Thirdly, we use the concept of *emergence* to argue that the higher-order skill which is the goal of learning (for example, communicative language ability) is something qualitatively different from, and irreducible to, its parts – that is, the linguistic elements which make up the curriculum (see also section 1.3, Sayer 1992:119). This raises problems for a componential view of learning.

Given our primary interest in language learning the more holistic, learner-oriented nature of the social constructivist approach, and the central role of social interaction, seems more relevant to our purpose than the more componential, knowledge-oriented nature of the cognitive constructivist approach.

So-called cognitive development models (Shavelson 2008, 2009) propose fixed progression routes through bodies of learning material. Shavelson warns against premature applications of such models, citing research to counter the assumption that cognitive development is neatly describable, or follows predictable paths. Successful formative assessment is difficult to reduce to rules, he concludes, and depends on a high level of teacher expertise. The social constructivist emphasis on process over product – learning *as* classroom interaction, rather than as an *outcome* of it – has proved a powerful concept in developing the model of learning-oriented assessment presented in this volume.

3.3 Task-based interaction

Having located Learning Oriented Assessment within a social constructivist paradigm, let us analyse in more detail the nature of learning-oriented classroom interaction.

Interaction is at the heart of learning. Vygotsky (1986) views all cognition as socially constructed, so that learning happens through interaction with a more knowing other (e.g. a teacher) and what a learner can achieve with assistance defines the *zone of proximal development*: the achievable learning space. According to Vygotsky, 'every function in the child's cultural development appears twice: . . . first between people (interpsychological) and then inside the child (intrapsychological)' (1978:57).

We may compare Vygotsky's position with that of Krashen (1982), who proposes that learning happens by exposure to comprehensible input, at a level just beyond the learner's current capacity (the *i+1 level*). Krashen takes a Chomskyan view of language acquisition as an innate capacity: a specifically programmed Language Acquisition Device (LAD). Formal language teaching is not necessary, and indeed Krashen goes so far as to claim that it does not work. The two notions of the i+1 level and the zone of proximal development seem at first glance to be similar, but in fact they are quite different: while the LAD that Krashen appeals to is a black box which eludes closer study, Vygotsky provides an interaction-based theory of learning which can be productively implemented. We have noted Vygotsky's influence on, for example, the Assessment for Learning Group in the UK (Black and Wiliam 2003), and the dynamic assessment movement in the USA (Lantolf and Poehner 2011).

Within language learning the importance of interaction has also been identified, although Vygotsky's influence has impacted on how SLA conceptions are now understood: 'it has shifted the emphasis from viewing interaction as leading to language learning to interaction as being the place where language learning actually occurs' (Ellis and Barkhuizen 2005:251).

Thus Swain's (1985) 'output hypothesis' argues that production and practice is necessary for the self-monitoring which enables the learner to test and modify hypotheses about the language. But more recently Swain (2001:281) actually defines learning in terms of interaction: 'learning is understood to be a continuous process of constructing and extending meaning that occurs during learners' involvement in situated joint activities'.

The literature on interaction refers to a number of concepts – *tasks, goals, scaffolding, feedback* and more – which help us define models of learning-oriented assessment. The following sections review some of these concepts.

3.3.1 Tasks

A task-based approach to language education follows naturally from the social constructivist position presented in section 3.1. As noted in section 4.2, the concept of task occupies a central place in the CEFR's action-oriented model. Van den Branden (Ed) (2006:7) compares a number of definitions of task-based learning offered by different authors:

- an activity which required learners to arrive at an outcome from given information through some process of thought and which allowed teachers to control and regulate that process was regarded as a task (Prabhu 1987)
- a piece of classroom work which involves learners in comprehending, manipulating, producing or interacting in the target language while their attention is primarily focused on meaning rather than form (Nunan 1989)

- one of a set of differentiated, sequenceable, problem-posing activities involving learners' cognitive and communicative procedures applied to existing and new knowledge in the collective exploration and pursuance of foreseen or emergent goals within a social milieu (Candlin 1987)
- an activity in which:

  – meaning is primary
  – there is some communication problem to solve
  – there is some sort of relationship to comparable real-world activities
  – task completion has some priority
  – the assessment of the task is in terms of outcome (Skehan 1998)

- an activity, influenced by learner choice, and susceptible to learner reinterpretation, which requires learners to use language, with emphasis on meaning, to attain an objective (Bygate, Skehan and Swain (Eds) 2001).

These authors highlight different (and to an extent conflicting) aspects of task-based learning: Prabhu stresses outcomes, and allows the teacher a controlling influence; Nunan stresses the learner's attention to meaning; for Candlin it is the socially situated nature of the event which is foremost; Skehan additionally mentions a degree of real-world authenticity. Bygate et al alone stress the role of the learners in interpreting objectives and controlling outcomes.

Our essential definition of task, which aligns with a social constructivist view, is that it leads to the *purposeful use of language to communicate personally significant meanings.*

Tasks may or may not provide the organising principle for a context of instructed learning; but the implications of adopting a task-based approach is that learning is conceived in more holistic, functional and communicative terms than is the case with a linguistically organised syllabus. To this extent a task-based approach is more in line with SLA views of how languages are actually learned (Van den Branden (Ed) 2006:9).

Nonetheless, Van den Branden finds task-based teaching to be consistent with the grammatically oriented concept of *focus on form*, and cites recent SLA research which supports such an approach.

3.3.2 Supporting learners' performance on tasks

Prior knowledge

The importance of building on prior knowledge is well expressed in Ausubel's principle of contingent teaching: 'The most important single factor influencing learning is what the learner already knows; ascertain this and teach him accordingly' (1968:vi, in James and Pedder 2006). Clearly, each learner can only move forward from where they are. If a classroom exercise assumes certain prior knowledge, a first step is to begin with a check on whether students possess that knowledge. Shepard (2000:10) states that 'prior knowledge and feedback are two well-established ideas, the meaning of which may have to be re-examined as learning theories are changed to take better account of social and cultural contexts'. That is, learners may have different experiences, understanding, goals and conceptions which ideally the teacher should be able to identify and respond to.

Explicit criteria

'Sharing criteria with learners' is one of the four fundamental principles of formative assessment proposed by Black and Wiliam (1998b) and others working with performance assessment in education. It is the basis for learners to develop the ability to self-assess. According to Frederiksen and Collins (1989:30) students must be helped to develop an awareness of the important characteristics of good problem-solving, good writing etc., and of the habits of mind which contribute to achieving these. Students should know what will count as good performance on the task.

Scaffolding

Shepard (2000) describes instructional scaffolding as interactive feedback provided in ways that reflect constructivist principles of learning. Scaffolding is defined by Wood, Bruner and Ross (1976:90) as a process 'that enables a child or novice to solve a task or achieve a goal that would be beyond his unassisted efforts'. Effective scaffolding techniques are reported to include:

- highlighting learning strategies to the learner, for example reconstructing how a goal was achieved (Maloch 2002)
- structuring the task's level of difficulty, jointly participating in problem-solving, focusing the learner's attention to the task, and motivating the learner (Rogoff 1997)
- varying the level of help provided; the help is calibrated to the student's level of performance: 'It is not simply intervening that makes a difference to learning because just any kind of help will not do' (Rodgers 2004:506)
- providing opportunities for errors as errors are necessary for learning
- repetition, contextual embedding, drawing connections between lessons or classroom activities, thereby altering the cognitive complexity of the activity with reference to learner needs (Rea-Dickins 2006).

Effective scaffolding requires the teacher to have knowledge of the task (e.g. what is involved in learning to read) and knowledge of the student (knowing where the student is in their learning). The teacher must also decide what errors to attend to and what level of help to provide (Wood et al 1976).

There are forms of assessment which appeal explicitly to the notion of scaffolding in order to measure language ability interactively within the zone of proximal development. Lantolf and Poehner (2011) describe an interventionist dynamic assessment procedure whereby performance on a task is scored on the basis of how many clues or prompts the student requires in order to succeed on the task. From a slightly different perspective, Pollitt and Ahmed (2004) propose a similar 'support model' for summative school examinations, arguing that a response elicited through prompting gives a more valid measure of a lower-level student's ability than the zero response observed if that student is unable to engage with the task at all.

Although the term 'scaffolding' as used above refers to classroom interaction, a similar concept is evident in all contexts of task-based communication. In the social world the role of the interlocutor frequently plays a crucial role in scaffolding successful communication, something which complicates attempts to assess communicative language ability as if it were purely a property of the learner. The construction of effective test tasks also involves a form of scaffolding to adjust the level of difficulty appropriately. This aspect of scaffolding is further discussed in section 8.2.

Goals

The goals of learning are of course framed at higher and more formal levels, enshrined in curricula and course materials; but what is important in completing a task is how the goals are viewed by the participants (teachers and learners) in the interaction. Black and Wiliam (1998a:20) state that:

> The core of the activity of formative assessment lies in the sequence of two actions. The first is the perception by the learner of a gap between a desired goal and his or her present state (of knowledge, and/or understanding, and/or skill). The second is the action taken by the learner to close that gap in order to attain the desired goal (Ramaprasad 1983, Sadler 1989).

Goals may be set by the teacher, but importantly may also be constructed by the learner. James and Pedder (2006) refer to a distinction between *learning* or *mastery* goals and *performance* goals. The first characterises the goal orientation of learners who 'strive to increase their competence, to understand or master something new'; the second learners who 'strive either to document, or gain favourable judgements of, their competence or to avoid negative judgments of their competence' (Dweck 1989:88–89). Black and Wiliam (1998a:23) describe two such groups:

> The former spoke of the importance of learning, believed in the value of effort to achieve mastery, and had a generally positive attitude to learning. The latter attributed failure to lack of ability, spoke more in

terms of their relative ability . . . and focused on the significance of out-performing others.

This psychological perspective is coherent with Butler's (1987) *task-involving* and *ego-involving* properties of evaluations (see section 3.3.3), Lepper and Hodell's (1989) *intrinsic* and *extrinsic* reward systems, or Black and Wiliam's (1998a) distinction between *process* and *product* goals.

As noted earlier, summative assessment has been criticised for focusing learners' (and teachers') attention on performance rather than learning goals, with the consequent risk that learners develop the characteristics of *learned helplessness* over *resilience* (Dweck 2000).

The literature reviewed above confirms that a variety of personal features – self-concept, self-attribution, self-efficacy, and assumptions about the nature of learning – will impact positively or negatively on learning; and consequently that forms of feedback must be carefully considered, to discourage students from adopting performance-oriented goals that seek approval rather than pursue learning (James and Pedder 2006), and to encourage positive beliefs about ability and effort.

3.3.3 Feedback on task performance

Shepard (2000) interprets scaffolding as feedback based on constructivist principles; but the term feedback itself goes back literally to the origins of formative assessment. For Bloom, who first applied the term to students, the purpose of formative evaluation was 'to provide feedback and correctives at each stage in the teaching-learning process' (Bloom1969:48, in Bennett 2011). Black and Wiliam (1998a) also consider the concepts of formative assessment and of feedback to overlap strongly, hence the considerable space given to it in their study. They cite Ramaprasad's (1983) definition: 'Feedback is information about the gap between the actual level and the reference level of a system parameter which is used to alter the gap in some way' (Black and Wiliam 1998a:4).

Ramaprasad stresses that if the information is not actually used in altering the gap, then there is no feedback. Black and Wiliam (1998a) conclude that the quality of feedback is critical. Feedback is most effective when it is designed to stimulate correction of errors through a thoughtful approach to them in relation to the original learning relevant to the task. Effective feedback focuses on deep rather than shallow learning (see section 3.3.4, and Wiggins 1998).

However, there is evidence that learners respond to feedback differently, making it more difficult to identify what constitutes good feedback. Kluger and DeNisi (1996) identify four typical responses to a 'feedback–standard discrepancy': learners may attempt to reach the standard, if they have high commitment and self-belief, or abandon the standard completely, if their self-belief is low (Dweck's 'learned helplessness'), or change the standard, or simply deny that the feedback–standard gap exists.

These findings agree with a study by Butler (1988), a surprising result of which was that giving grades as feedback could nullify the positive impact of giving comments on the task. See also Butler and Neuman (1995).

The Black and Wiliam (1998a) account of feedback has subsequently been challenged or extended in several ways. For example, Shepard (2000:11) asserts that 'the existing literature on feedback will be of limited value to us in reconceptualizing assessment from a constructivist perspective, because the great majority of existing studies are based on behaviorist assumptions'. Shepard proposes that social mediation of learning can occur within groups of students, and insists that this social constructivist perspective provides a view of motivation profoundly different from behaviourist reinforcement.

3.3.4 Aspects of learning

Transfer

Shepard (2000) sees a close relationship between truly understanding a concept and being able to transfer knowledge and use it in new situations. In contrast to memorisation, true understanding is flexible, connected, and generalisable. These notions overlap with the concept of deep learning discussed in the next section.

Deep and shallow learning

Learning with understanding, or *deep learning* (Entwistle and Entwistle 1991, Marton, Hounsell and Entwistle (Eds) 1984) is invoked by Harlen and James (1997) to characterise the difference between formative and summative assessment: deep learning is the goal of formative assessment, they claim, while shallow learning is held to be the result of preparing for summative assessments. According to Harlen and James (1997:368) deep learning implies:

> . . . an intention to develop personal understanding, active interaction with the content, particularly in relating new ideas to previous knowledge and experience, linking ideas together using integrating principles, and relating evidence to conclusions.

Deep learning is 'owned by the learner in the sense that it becomes a fundamental part of the way he or she understands the world' (Harlen and James 1997:368). Facilitating deep learning is seen as the essence of formative assessment. This distinction relates to the notion of *emergence* discussed next.

3.3.5 Emergence

Emergence is an important concept within this text. It describes the fundamental, qualitative step-change between conscious learning of the elements of a language – grammar, vocabulary – and the emergence of a higher-order system which is qualitatively different from, and irreducible to, its parts (Larsen-Freeman and Cameron 2008, Sayer 1992:119). When the term 'higher order' or 'lower order' is used in this volume it relates explicitly to the notion of emergence.

There are important implications for pedagogy. The emergence of communicative language ability cannot be explained in terms of simple content transmission. Thus we should not expect the higher-order objectives to be achieved solely by a presentation, practice, performance (PPP) approach to teaching. Such an approach assumes that the whole is just the sum of its parts, whereas the higher-order system is significantly more than that. Therefore there must be an important place in the learning-oriented classroom for interactions that specifically promote the emergence of the higher-order skill.

We may illustrate the distinction between lower and higher-order skills by looking critically at a description of classroom-based learning-oriented assessment by the Assessment Reform Group (2002:2):

> Much of what teachers and learners do in classrooms can be described as assessment. That is, tasks and questions prompt learners to demonstrate their knowledge, understanding and skills. What learners say and do is then observed and interpreted, and judgments are made about how learning can be improved. These assessment processes are an essential part of everyday classroom practice and involve both teachers and learners in reflection, dialogue and decision making.

The activity described above might be understood in two quite different ways: one focused on learners and their developing cognition, the other on transmitting the content of learning.

What is clear here is that teachers and learners are seen as active agents in constructing learning interactions, even if the teacher, as the more knowing interlocutor, has a greater role in organising their implementation. What is not clear is the level of cognition which is supposed to be engaged by learning interactions: at a *metacognitive* level interaction seems to be driven by the teacher's didactic intention, so that the 'reflection, dialogue and decision making' might focus, for example, on identifying, discussing and correcting errors made by the students. But at the *cognitive* level we can see learning being driven by learners' purposeful use of language to communicate personally significant meanings, given the engaging context and scaffolding supplied by the teacher. This is where learning happens, according to the insights offered by social constructivist learning theory and reflected in the

CEFR's action-oriented model of learning. If cognition is not engaged at this level then the teacher's orchestration of learning interaction will most likely prove ineffective (see section 5.1.2 for a discussion on learning and personal development).

3.4 Roles of teachers and learners

What the concepts discussed above have in common is that they all relate to learning interaction. Learning interaction addresses a task, has a goal, deals in meanings, may be mediated and scaffolded, has outcomes, leading to reflection and evaluation, and engages and changes cognition, i.e. produces learning. We should not think of these concepts as tools, methods, techniques or procedures for promoting learning: as Vygotsky argues, they *are* learning in action.

The major participants in interaction are learners and teachers, but primarily learners, because they are where the learning happens. Learning can only build on the learner's prior experience, and a common situation is that both learners and teachers come to the task already negatively conditioned by previous experience. In the language of international educational surveys, there may exist powerful *antecedent* conditions – part of the context in which education proceeds. International surveys like to focus on the *malleable* factors, amenable to change, such as curricula, methodology or incentives for teachers, but both kinds of factor impact on the educational outcomes which surveys measure.

Therefore good learners and teachers are not produced simply by following some set of effective procedures. In many contexts there are antecedent issues to deal with: not a question of education so much as re-education. Examples of such issues in different contexts are given in the next section.

3.4.1 The learner

Sadler (1998, reported by Shepard 2000:14), in an Australian context, comments on the difficulty of remedying 'the long-term exposure of students to defective patterns of formative assessment'. Perrenoud (1998), in a Swiss context, notes that while there are always certain students in a class who are willing to work harder and engage with formative assessment, other children and adolescents are 'imprisoned in the identity of a bad pupil and an opponent' (1998:92). According to Perrenoud, 'every teacher who wants to practice formative assessment must reconstruct the teaching contract so as to counteract the habits acquired by his pupils' (1998:92).

This underlines the importance of enabling learners to acquire a positive image of themselves as learners. Shepard (2000:10) cites Lave and Wenger's (1991) concept of legitimate peripheral participation, whereby 'learning and development of an identity of mastery occur together as a newcomer becomes increasingly adept at participating in a community of practice'. The social constructivist classroom should offer the ideal context for developing a more positive disposition to learning. The discussion of learning objectives in section 5.1 finds the most important objectives, in terms of long-term achievement, to be the skills and dispositions of *learning how to learn*, which include developing feelings of membership and inclusion in the group where learning takes place.

Writing in a higher education context, Boud (2000) and Boud and Falchikov (2006) take further the implications for assessment and learning goals of needing to prepare students to become members of communities of practice. In an increasingly complex world they foresee challenges that will not be addressed by disciplinary or interdisciplinary knowledge, where problems will require the combining of expertise in new ways, and propose that 'a third purpose of assessment – assessment to foster learning throughout life – be given equal attention alongside the well-established purposes of assessment for certification and assessment to aid current learning' (Boud and Falchikov 2006:400).

Self- and peer-assessment

Good learning requires learners to become autonomous and capable of self-direction. The ability to self-assess is a necessary aspect of this. As noted previously, giving learners explicit criteria for what counts as high-quality or successful completion of a task is critical for developing the capacity to self-assess. Sadler (1989) asserts that students' understandings can only change if they can understand the goals which they are failing to attain, locate their own position in relation to those goals, and then pursue learning which changes their understanding. Thus self-assessment is essential for effective learning.

Peer- and self-assessment are among the four clusters of classroom practices identified by Black and Wiliam (1998a) as being effective in enhancing learning and achievement: peer-assessment is 'an important complement [to] and may even be a prior requirement for self-assessment' (James and Pedder 2006:116, citing Black, Harrison, Lee, Marshall and Wiliam 2003:50).

Peer-assessment should be effective where learners are prepared to treat learning as a joint activity: 'the power of peer-assessment, especially in contexts of strong learning orientation (Watkins, Carnell, Lodge, Wagner and Whalley 2000), rests on an assumption of co-agency in the collaborative construction of knowledge' (James and Pedder 2006:116).

Motivation

Motivation for learning, although not directly linked to achievement, has been shown to influence students' willingness to persist with learning when it becomes difficult and their willingness to work hard at it (Csizér and Dörnyei 2005, Gardner 1985). A better understanding of what motivates learners may inform instructional decisions such as selecting resources, planning learning activities, etc. In a language context motivation has been conceptualised as composed of several components, including:

- **instrumentality**: belief in the usefulness of gaining proficiency in the language
- **attitudes** towards the target language community, such as a desire to visit countries that use the target language or interest in having contact with speakers of that language
- **milieu**: support for language learning from the learners' immediate social environment (i.e. family and friends)
- **linguistic self-confidence**: confidence level in the target language
- **cultural interest**: appreciation of the target language communities' cultural products (i.e. music, movies, etc.)
- **integrativeness**: desire to integrate into the target language culture.

More recently newer versions of motivation (e.g. Dörnyei 2006) have incorporated some of these into the concept of the *idealised self-image* and its constituent parts. The idealised self-image – how learners want to see themselves – clearly relates to social constructivist concepts of group membership.

Large-scale assessment poses threats to motivation, as extrinsic or instrumental motivation to perform well in an assessment, when this is perceived as high stakes, may replace intrinsic motivation in the subject, with a negative impact on learning. Perhaps encouraged by the immediate milieu that places high value in achieving a particular test score, learners may be motivated to achieve that score at any cost, rather than learning the language. Negative consequences in these cases can include learners cramming to memorise test items and a higher incidence of malpractice and cheating.

3.4.2 The teacher

The literature on formative assessment makes clear that the role of the teacher in learning-oriented assessment is critically important but also, in many contexts, very difficult. Antecedent conditions include factors such as government policy which focus undue attention on external high-stakes summative assessment. This may be impossible to change – in fact the very existence of the formative–summative distinction reflects a view of summative assessment as a necessary evil whose effects can, at best, be mitigated by finding a place for a separate learning-oriented assessment component. Several studies (Black et al 2003, James and Pedder 2006, Johnston, Guice, Baker, Malone and Michelson 1995, Turner 2006) attest to the difficulties that teachers experience in working to two different sets of objectives.

Other antecedent conditions may include teachers' own long-standing beliefs and assumptions about teaching, which are difficult but perhaps not impossible to change.

The teacher's role in learning

Most important of these perhaps is the locus of control in the classroom. As James and Pedder (2006:117) state: 'If the goal is to encourage students to become autonomous, independent, active learners, then the locus of control over learning needs to shift in many classrooms – from teachers to students.' Typically, successful learning is reflected in such a transfer of responsibility from the teacher to the learner.

In order to change beliefs and accustomed practice in such fundamental ways, James and Pedder (2006) claim that teachers must come to understand classroom-based learning-oriented assessment in terms of its underlying principles. As the title of the paper *Beyond method* implies, teachers must look beyond a particular set of classroom techniques and methods. Changing practice begins with changing beliefs, rather than vice versa.

Social constructivist principles would lead teachers to share responsibility for the practice of classroom teaching and assessment with students. Moreover, teachers should be ready to accept the same feedback and critique of their own work as that which is expected of students (Shepard 2000:12). James and Pedder (2006:111) argue similarly. The implication for professional development is that teachers need opportunities to examine critically the values and beliefs that shape their practice (see Appendix 3 for James and Pedder's (2006) five hypotheses on assessment for learning).

The teacher's role in classroom assessment

As Rea-Dickins (2006) points out, CBA tends to serve several competing agendas: supporting the language development of individual learners, covering curriculum content, and/or gathering data for formal reporting. In the context of working in England, Teasdale and Leung (2000) find a lack of clarity about the theoretical frameworks which are invoked. The several roles of the teacher in assessment are left weakly identified by an 'uneasy articulation of different principles underpinning psychometric measurement and pedagogy' (Teasdale and Leung 2000:163).

Rea-Dickins (2006:167) offers a detailed analysis of how teachers' classroom discourse changes to reflect different assessment roles: as more formal 'raters' of learner performance, identifying levels of language achievement; or as agents of a more learning-oriented 'ongoing appraisal of students through the ebb and flow of classroom discourse'. She concludes that when teachers are in 'teaching' or 'curriculum-tracking' mode they might miss opportunities for learners to engage and to develop their language. 'What appears crucial is not that all assessment should ideally be formative but that teachers are able to provide for their learners a balance in the types of assessment within instruction. An overemphasis on patterns of assessment where learners are cued to display their language knowledge is undesirable' (Rea-Dickins 2006:184).

For teachers to fulfil such a range of roles they require professional training and support, which seems frequently to be lacking. Accordingly, a literature has grown up on how teachers can be equipped with the necessary assessment skills. For example, Brindley (2001) advances a model of how practical technical and professional support could be provided to teachers in order to develop more professional assessment competences.

There is the concept of *assessment literacy*. In its basic form this might involve training in assessment to equip the users of external assessments to understand their intended uses, to evaluate them critically and to be aware of their limitations, e.g. in terms of the information they provide (Inbar-Lourie 2008, Taylor 2009).

Such an understanding might also be a starting point for teachers to develop more advanced knowledge and skills, including their own ability to construct various kinds of assessment. However, it is clear that assessment literacy for teachers must distinguish summative from learning-oriented assessment.

Brindley (2001:403) stresses the need for better professional development, pointing out that 'the skills required for classroom assessment which is embedded in the curriculum are quite different from those that are conventionally taught in "educational measurement" courses (e.g. Arter 1999, Brookhart 1999, Stiggins 1999, Whittington 1999)'. In the US the National Council for Accreditation of Teacher Education/American Council on the Teaching of Foreign Languages (NCATE/ACTFL) and NCATE/TESOL teacher development standards give significant attention to teachers' competence in assessment.

The teacher's role in summative assessment

As we saw in section 2.2.3, there are many contexts where teachers are being given a very significant role – even a decisive one – in summative assessment. The impact is particularly dramatic in the case of languages, which reflects the twin revolutions of the 'communicative turn' and of formative assessment. The first of these, most clearly visible in the wide adoption of the CEFR (Council of Europe 2001), stresses that the purpose of language education is to equip learners to communicate. Formative assessment puts classroom discourse at the centre of learning and asserts its primary importance. Clearly, the two movements have much in common.

The new focus on functional language skills and on teachers as the orchestrators of their development represents in many contexts a radical change that exerts great strains on the system: see for example Davison and Hamp-Lyons

(2009) and Davison and Leung (2009) on the development of an SBA component in various international educational systems, treated more fully in section 2.2.3.

In many other countries attempts to give teachers a greater role in assessment still come up against the dominant role of large-scale summative testing. In the context of England we have noted the ARG's critical stance towards formal, summative assessment, and consequently there is some disagreement as to whether, or how, teachers should be involved in doing it. Black and Wiliam (1998a) refer to a debate between those who draw attention to the difficulties of combining the two roles of formative and summative assessment (Harlen, Gipps, Broadfoot and Nuttall 1992, Scott 1991, Simpson 1990) and those who argue that it can and indeed must be done to escape the dominance of external summative testing (Black 1993, Harlen 2005, 2009, Mansell et al 2009, Wiliam and Black 1996).

Thus, for example, Mansell et al (2009) make strong claims for the positive role that teachers could play in the assessment of learning. Harlen (2005:221) asserts that current assessments provide information of low validity and reliability, and at significant cost: 'moderation of teachers' judgements . . . can be conducted so that it not only serves a quality control function, but also has an impact on the process of assessment by teachers, having a quality assurance function as well.'

3.5 In summary

This chapter has attempted a broad review of the literature on learning and formative assessment, introducing social constructivism as an appropriate model for Learning Oriented Assessment, particularly for the case of languages.

Learning is a product of social interaction. Tasks which motivate interaction, in the classroom or in the context of an assessment, therefore play a key role in the Learning Oriented Assessment approach. We presented a range of definitions of tasks, and provided our own definition of the task as an activity which leads to *the purposeful use of language to communicate personally significant meanings*. The conditions for conducting classroom tasks so as to enable learning to happen include:

- ensuring that learners have the necessary prior knowledge
- sharing explicit criteria for success
- skilled scaffolding of learners' performance, producing learning interaction
- ensuring that in approaching the task learners adopt goals which focus on learning rather than on gaining favourable judgements of their competence.

After attempting a task, feedback is the essential part of the assessment cycle which enables learning. One indication that learning has taken place is that the learner can *transfer* a competence acquired during task completion to a different context. This relates to the notion of *deep and shallow learning*, and to the important concept of *emergence*: the ability to use language to communicate emerges as a higher-order skill, which is not a simple product of curricular objectives. This implies that there must be a place in the language classroom for both curriculum-centred and learner-centred work.

Considering the roles of teachers and learners, Learning Oriented Assessment aims at enabling learners to:

- overcome any prior negative experiences of language learning
- feel part of a community of practice, developing a positive disposition to learning
- in consequence, develop attitudes and dispositions which enable them to become good learners.

The capacity for peer-assessment and self-assessment is important for learning, as is developing positive, intrinsic motivation to learn. Teachers may also have long-standing beliefs and assumptions about teaching, which are difficult but perhaps not impossible to change. Significant transfer of responsibility from the teacher to the learner is characteristic of the learning-oriented classroom. Teachers may have different roles and duties concerning teaching, assessment and reporting, which are difficult to separate out. Training in assessment literacy will be of value.

4 What is language learning?

'There's all the difference in the world between having something to say, and having to say something.'

The School and Society (John Dewey 1915:35)

In this volume we present Learning Oriented Assessment as a general approach to education; but our specific interest is in languages. It is also true that Learning Oriented Assessment is particularly relevant to language learning, given that language is both the medium and the goal of learning. In essence, language is a special case. It is unique among school subjects in the range of knowledge and skills involved in the learning and the number of learner attributes it engages in the process.

4.1 Languages as a special case

In education languages play several roles:

- as '*first*' languages, which are key to personal growth, and developing literacy, affording access to both 'broad' and 'high' aspects of a society's cultural capital
- as '*foreign*' languages, which promote explicit or implicit understanding of language as a meaning-making system, and which offer access to culture in the wider world
- as the *language of schooling*, which is essential in order to learn any school subjects, and any deficit in which will impact on the learning achievements of non-native speakers and native speakers alike.

Any intervention in a particular context of language learning should recognise these several aspects of languages across the curriculum.

Cumming (2009:91) points out that language education serves a wider range of societal purposes than does the standard stuff of primary through secondary education. Acquiring and demonstrating some prescribed level of language ability is now a high-stakes issue for would-be immigrants in many regions of the world. More generally it is key to mobility in the international workplace and for higher education.

For the children of immigrants and refugees, a high level of competence in the language of education in a given country is a pre-requisite for achieving academic success, with all that this implies for their future. Thus for many learners within and outside the standard educational cycle language competences represent a vital skill to acquire.

A second distinguishing feature relates precisely to the nature of language ability as a skill, or rather, a complex set of skills. Language is unique among school subjects in the range of learner attributes – cognitive, psycho-motor and affective – which it engages (Coleman 2004).

Davison and Leung (2009:401) consider that TBA has several advantages over external examinations, especially in assessing language, 'because effective language development requires not just knowledge but skill and application in a wide range of situations and modes of communication'. They liken language to other performance-based subjects such as music, art, drama, and various vocational subjects.

Several conclusions follow from this. Ability in languages is not uniquely acquired in schools, but also by use in the world outside school. What is learned does not necessarily reflect what is in the curriculum. Language is probably not best taught by attempting to reduce it to an inventory of content, even though that is what many educational systems may do, in line with the treatment of other school subjects. The concepts associated with *learning how to learn* are nowhere more critical than in languages, and nowhere – potentially – more readily acquired.

4.2 The Common European Framework of Reference for Languages

The CEFR for languages is an influential document published by the Council of Europe in 2001, which offers two things:

- a presentation of communication as the goal of language learning within a multilingual Europe based on intercultural understanding, and of how this goal might be achieved within formal language education
- a descriptive framework of levels of language proficiency, enabling all languages and contexts of learning to develop a common understanding of what it means to master a language at a given level.

It is probably fair to say that most users of the CEFR are more familiar with the descriptive framework, but here we will focus on the discussion of language teaching.

The text of the CEFR betrays its multiple authorship: if we look in it for a view on the nature of language learning we will find a range of influences:

- the functional/notional approach of Wilkins, also reflected in the Waystage–Threshold–Vantage series by van Ek and Trim
- the needs-analysis approach that follows from John Trim's work on a unit-credit system for adult learners

- the behavioural scaling descriptive approach of Brian North's scales
- the chapter on task-based learning
- Daniel Coste's notion of the action-oriented approach.

Of these it is the action-oriented model which most clearly reflects social constructivist notions. It is also coherent with the work done by Cambridge English to develop constructs for the four skills of listening, speaking, reading and writing, based on Weir's (2005b) *socio-cognitive* validation model. Focusing on cognition, the socio-cognitive model is coherent with Coste's action-oriented approach and it adds substance to the description of the CEFR levels, remedying early criticisms of the descriptive framework. Corpus-based work within English Profile (Hawkins and Filipović 2012) has contributed a further, linguistic dimension to the CEFR levels for English.

The action-oriented model for language use and learning is described as involving:

> ... the actions performed by persons who as individuals and as social agents develop a range of *competences*, both *general* and in particular *communicative language competences*. They draw on the competences at their disposal in various contexts under various *conditions* and *constraints* to engage in *language activities* involving *language processes* to produce and/or receive *texts* in relation to *themes* in specific *domains*, activating those *strategies* which seem most appropriate for carrying out the *tasks* to be accomplished. The monitoring of these actions by the participants leads to the reinforcement or modification of their competences (Council of Europe 2001:9, emphases in original).

This paragraph describes a learner's cognition developing through engagement with communicative tasks that arise in social interaction. It is a socio-cognitive model of language use – cognition is manifested in, and develops through, social interaction.

The CEFR's *general competences* mentioned in the above paragraph are particularly interesting. They comprise:

- knowledge, i.e. declarative knowledge (*savoir*)
- skills and know-how (*savoir-faire*)
- existential competence (*savoir-être*)
- ability to learn (*savoir apprendre*) (Council of Europe 2001).

These are recognisably social constructivist concepts, and as they answer our second question: *what is to be learned?* we will come back to them in Chapter 5.

4.3 Natural language acquisition

The most striking fact about languages is that most people acquire their first one at an early age, quickly and in some sense 'perfectly'. Throughout the history of language teaching there have been attempts to teach second or foreign languages in the same way, in contrast to the objectified study of grammar characteristic of teaching Latin or Greek in 'grammar' schools. For the wealthy, going abroad to learn a language, or having a native-speaker tutor, were effective options. Modern-day immersion learning programmes are comparable, but are feasible only in a few special contexts, such as learning French in Canada.

Can such an acquisition-oriented approach work in school? The social constructivist model seems to come closer to an acquisition approach in stressing the importance of meaning-making through purposeful interaction. Furthermore, technology has made it possible to bring any amount of authentic language into the classroom, enabling far more exposure to natural language. However, the study of language as a formal system whose rules need to be mastered is still generally an intrinsic feature of languages in school.

This is not a bad thing: within the limitations of formal schooling a wholly natural acquisition approach is barely feasible; and there is an argument that becoming familiar with grammar is an enabling skill that may pay dividends in learning further languages. However, what is missing is a theory of learning to relate natural acquisition and formal learning in a systemic way. The view of learning which we will develop in this volume will attempt to contribute to this (see section 7.4).

4.4 Second Language Acquisition research

SLA is a broad, interdisciplinary area of research, encompassing both foreign language learning in formal settings and acquisition of a second language in an informal setting (the distinction is not strongly marked). This brief review looks at several accounts of how languages are learned, chiefly seeking to add further detail to the picture of learning provided by the socio-cognitive model which we have adopted.

4.4.1 Processing accounts

Input processing is a distinctive strand within SLA associated with VanPatten (1996, 2004 (Ed), 2007, 2008). It has generated a rigorous research agenda around instructional applications. Input processing is not in itself a complete model of SLA but addresses one aspect of it.

There is ample evidence that learners do not always pick up elements present in oral or written input. The central question of the field of input processing is: 'What linguistic data do learners process in the input and what constrains or guides that processing?' Research on these issues has led to the formulation of a set of principles intended to explain the driving forces and constraints of input processing by learners. By way of illustration, these principles include:

- *Definition of processing*: processing refers to making a connection between form and meaning/function. According to this principle, processing differs from *perception* or *noticing*, which do not require learners to make a form–meaning connection when encountering a new form. So, a learner may notice the inflection *-ing* at the end of verbs but not process a form–meaning connection.

- *Primacy of content words*: learners process content words in the input before anything else. This principle stems from a learner's fundamental need to derive meaning out of input. In the early stages of acquisition learners will use the easiest and most efficient strategies to arrive at an interpretation, and that means focusing on lexical forms (Clahsen and Felser 2006, Gass 2003, Klein 1986, Truscott and Sharwood Smith 2004).

- *Lexical preference principle*: If grammatical forms express a meaning that can also be encoded lexically (e.g. that grammatical marker is redundant), then learners will not initially process those grammatical forms until they have lexical forms to which they can match them. This principle explains the delay seen in learners' processing and acquiring of what might be called redundant grammatical items (e.g. Ellis 1994, Gass and Selinker 2008).

These principles, which confirm the importance of meanings in processing input, have been exploited in a pedagogical intervention known as 'processing instruction' which in turn has generated a series of empirical studies.

4.4.2 Complexity theory

The key concept within complexity theory (CT) and related accounts (e.g. chaos theory, dynamic systems theory, emergentism) is that of a *complex system* which involves many interacting elements or parts (Ellis 1998, Gell-Mann 1992, Larsen-Freeman 1997, Larsen-Freeman and Cameron 2008, O'Grady 2005). This system adapts to new conditions as a result of feedback and it is influenced by its environment because it is 'open' to change. The system is typically characterised by organised complexity because the multiple 'parts work together to produce a coherent structure from their interaction, such as with individual birds coming together to form a flock . . . The structure emerges and is not dictated to or embedded in any one part' (Larsen-Freeman 2012:74).

CT sees language as a complex adaptive system which emerges from the interactions of its speakers when communicating with one another (Lee and Schumann 2005). The adaptive nature of language as a system means that the structures that ultimately emerge are those that fit the cognitive and motor capacities of the brain. The emergent form of the language, therefore, reflects the way it is used, not an innate mental programme (cf. Universal Grammar). 'Language itself is an ephiphenomenon of its speakers' (Larsen-Freeman 2012:75).

This view sees language development not merely 'as a process of acquiring abstract rules, but as the *emergence* of language abilities in *real time*' (Evans 2007:128). As Larsen-Freeman explains:

> Through encounters with others, a process of co-adaptation takes place, in which each interlocutor's language resources are shaped and reshaped through interaction . . . This socially situated view accords with an active view of the learner – someone who learns from positive evidence, while generating her own negative evidence from her active noticing and exploration of the bounds of the system (2012:76–77).

Larsen-Freeman (2012) offers implications for instruction. First, teaching is about *managing the dynamics of learning*, ensuring that the co-adaptation that takes place during classroom interactions promotes learning. Although teachers do not control learning, since learners carve their own path, teaching is still highly influential on learning: 'What a teacher can do is manage and serve her or his students' learning in a way that is consonant with their learning processes. Thus, any approach consonant with CT would not be curriculum-centered nor learner centered, but it would be learning-centered – where the learning guides the teaching and not vice versa' (Larsen-Freeman 2012:83).

Second, we should abandon inauthentic activities like traditional grammar drills. Larsen-Freeman advocates 'grammaring':

> [grammaring] involves using grammar structures accurately, meaningfully, and appropriately. Students learn to do this when they are engaged in practice activities that are psychologically authentic, with the conditions of learning aligned with the conditions of use, when they are provided with appropriately tuned feedback, and when the activities are deliberately interactive, not repetitive. In other words, from a CT perspective, language learning is seen as a process of meaningfully revisiting the same territory again and again, although each visit begins at a different starting point (2012:83).

Finally, CT calls for a more 'organic' syllabus that evolves with learners' readiness to learn a particular form. Such a syllabus would offer learners opportunities to engage in activities designed to encourage the use of particular forms. Teachers would diagnose the learner's readiness to learn a particular form or attend to forms that the learner avoids using.

All three implications about teaching and learning are consonant with the social constructivist approach at the heart of Learning Oriented Assessment.

4.4.3 Frequency-based accounts

Frequency-based accounts of language and SLA have their origins in structural linguistics (Saussure 1916) and the psychology of perception and processing (James 1890). Structural linguistics views language as 'an intermediary between thought and sound' (Saussure 1916:110). Linguistic signs are pairings of form and function and linguistic structure emerges from patterns of usage.

Frequency impacts on human perception. Psycholinguistic research has shown that language processing is also highly affected by usage frequency at all levels of language representation. From a psycholinguistic perspective, 'frequency is a key determinant of acquisition because "rules" of language, at all levels of analysis, from phonology, through syntax, to discourse are structural regularities which emerge from learners' lifetime analysis of the distributional characteristics of the language input' (Saussure 1916:110).

Frequency-based SLA approaches, then, conceptualise the problem of language learning as a problem of statistical sampling and estimation based on language usage. Ellis (2012) discusses implications for language teaching. For example, the *sample size* which L2 learners have to work with is often quite limited. Therefore some sort of selection and prioritisation of language usage may be desirable. Ellis contends that corpus and cognitive linguistic analyses can offer vital guidance as to which constructions are worthy of instruction, their relative frequency and the best examples for instruction and assessment. Genre analysis and needs analysis may help to identify constructions of most relevance to particular groups of learners; for example, by identifying relevant vocabulary for particular genres. Cognitive linguistics and psycholinguistics may complement this by providing guidance on how to order exemplars of a construction for optimal acquisition.

Finally, Ellis (2012:205) acknowledges that 'not everything that we can count in language counts in language cognition and acquisition' nor in the use of language in its social context. The associative learning of constructions as form–meaning pairings is ultimately affected by a combination of factors pertaining to language, cognition and social context.

4.4.4 The interaction of multiple principles in SLA: CASP

Based on empirical analyses of L2 data from the Cambridge Learner Corpus and inspired by work on complex adaptive systems (Gell-Mann 1992, Hawkins and Gell-Mann (Eds) 1992, Larsen-Freeman 1997), researchers within the English Profile Programme proposed a set of descriptive principles of SLA (see Filipović and Hawkins 2013 for the CASP model, Hawkins and Buttery 2009, Hawkins and Filipović 2012). These principles aim to account for SLA observed patterns and behaviours, such as relative sequencing in the acquisition of linguistic properties used by L2 learners, the presence or absence of transfer and the interaction and relative strength of SLA factors. The principles are concerned with syntactic and semantic phenomena and their learning and processing, that is, they are mainly linguistic and psycholinguistic in nature.

Figure 4.1 offers a graphical presentation of four general principles and four specific subprinciples that follow from them.

Figure 4.1 CASP general and specific principles

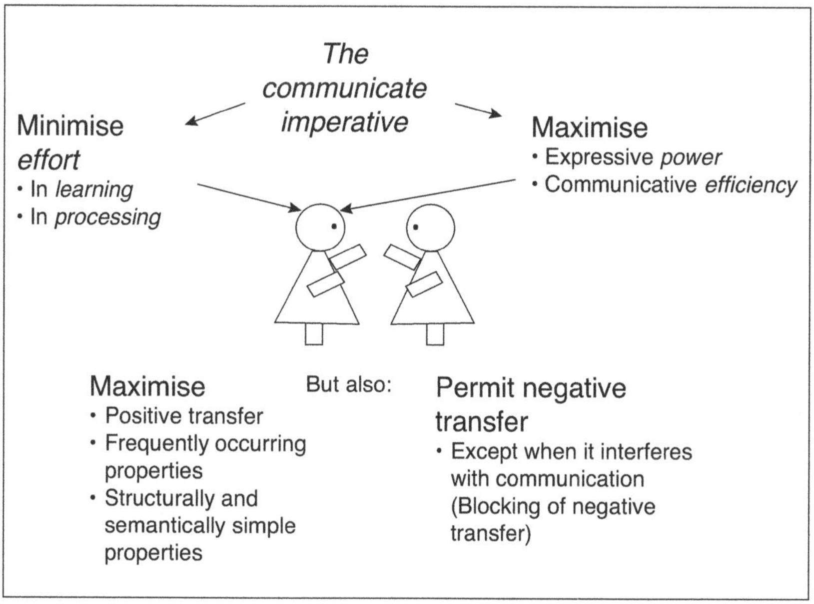

Altogether they define possible versus impossible and likely versus less likely acquisition stages, and are a first attempt to predict the relative sequence of observed learner data. For example, the general principle to *Minimise Learning Effort (MiL)* can be implemented in several ways:

- by transferring directly into the L2 grammatical and lexical properties common to L1 and L2, thereby exploiting pre-existing knowledge from the L1 (subprinciple 1: Maximise positive transfer)
- by using properties of the L2 which occur frequently, increasing their exposure and with it the ease of learning (subprinciple 2: Maximise frequently occurring properties)
- by preferring structural and semantic properties of the L2 which are simple rather than complex (subprinciple 3: Maximise structurally and semantically simple properties).

Additionally, the learning effort can be minimised by permitting negative transfer, leading to language errors, unless this interferes with communication, in which case this option is blocked.

The CASP principles predict specific features of language production, which can be confirmed in corpus data. They appear to illustrate in compelling fashion the link between learning and satisfying the need to communicate, which is at the heart of the learning-oriented model.

Conclusion

Although no particular SLA model or account captures the full range of factors and variables that shape SLA, they nonetheless offer some useful insights about how L2 learning works and how this knowledge can support and enhance language teaching and assessment. The major themes that emerge from this review can be summarised as follows:

- Language is a complex adaptive system, emerging gradually from usage and being shaped and reshaped by L2 learners through interaction with other speakers and co-adaptation.
- Multiple factors impact on L2 learning, from a range of fields of study including language, cognition and psychology, social context and pedagogy. Most SLA theorists are currently seeking to model the interactions among these multiple factors, and define what drives and constrains them.
- Teaching concerns managing the dynamics of learning and learner needs, facilitating the continuous reshaping and co-adaptation of L2 learner language. The curriculum should be learning oriented, with a flexible, 'organic' syllabus that evolves with learners' readiness for learning.
- Selection and ordering of language input and use may be desirable, taking into account factors including cognitive demand, frequency, appropriacy of examples, relevance and so on.
- L1 appears to play a significant role, aiding or impeding L2 learning.

Of the above conclusions, it is the treatment of language as a complex adaptive system which seems to align most closely with the social constructivist approach of Learning Oriented Assessment, and offer insight into how L2 learning takes place successfully in the classroom.

4.5 In summary

Languages are a special case in education, because language is the means through which all learning is mediated. Problems with mastering the language of schooling, including conventions of use in particular academic contexts, may be an issue not only for non-native speakers, such as migrant children, but also for native speakers.

Unlike other subjects, language is not uniquely acquired in schools, but also by use in the world outside school; what is to be learned cannot be fully laid down in a curriculum.

The CEFR presents an *action-oriented* approach to learning which is essentially social constructivist in nature. It describes a learner's language ability developing through engagement with communicative tasks that arise in social interaction. It is a *socio-cognitive* model of language use – cognition is manifested in, and develops through, social interaction.

We considered the process of 'natural' language acquisition through which everyone learns their first language. While this may not be practical for language learning in schools, we found that the social constructivist model seems to come close to an acquisition approach in the way that it stresses the importance of meaning-making through purposeful interaction as the driver of learning.

We briefly reviewed the field of SLA research in the hope of adding further detail to our picture of learning provided by the socio-cognitive model. Most relevant were the models based on CT, which recognise the dynamic nature of learning and model the way that language ability emerges through the effort of communicating.

5 What is to be learned?

'The goal of education is to enable individuals to continue their education.'

Democracy and Education (John Dewey 1916:100)

This chapter discusses three aspects to this question:

- the socially desired outcomes of learning
- the socio-cognitive *construct* of language proficiency (the *skills* to be acquired)
- the setting of curricular objectives (the *content* of learning).

The following sections address each of these aspects.

5.1 The desired outcomes of learning

The fundamental question at the heart of teaching and assessment is: what are the outcomes of learning which we wish to see? In the case of language learning there is a general consensus that the main objective should be to achieve a useful communicative competence in one or more languages. However, in a social constructivist view that objective is best achieved and maintained through life as part of a transformation of the learner's dispositions, attitudes and practical learning skills. A very positive outcome of learning would thus be that students acquire the valuable dispositions and life skills that enable them to continue learning throughout life. Whether or not this *outcome* can or should be made an explicit curricular *objective* is a different question; one to return to later in this volume.

The issue is that in a social constructivist approach learning and personal development seem to merge into one and the same process: these valuable auxiliary skills emerge from personal development, rather than explicit teaching. Languages are the clearest illustration of this. As successful language learners understand, each language learned to a good level adds a new dimension to their view of themselves and how they relate to and act in the world.

High-level statements of curricular objectives tend to frame goals in the most idealistic, humanistic terms. For example, the UK National Curriculum handbook states that:

... the school curriculum should develop enjoyment of, and commitment to, learning ... It should build on pupils' strengths, interests and experience and develop their confidence in their capacity to learn and work independently and collaboratively ... pass on enduring values, develop pupils' integrity and autonomy and help them to be responsible and caring citizens capable of contributing to the development of a just society ... (Department for Education and Employment/Qualifications and Curriculum Authority 1999:11).

Citing this statement, Harlen (2009:250) points to 'a strange contrast' between such rhetoric and what is actually assessed by tests. Perhaps this is slightly unfair, as important outcomes of learning may well not be directly measurable by tests, even though their indirect impact may be demonstrable and open to evaluation. Nonetheless, the contrast between the above ideals and the focus of most exam preparation is indeed striking.

James and Brown, writing from an ARG perspective, identify the following categories of learning outcome:

1. *Attainment*: often school curriculum based or measures of basic competence in the workplace.
2. *Understanding*: of ideas, concepts, processes.
3. *Cognitive and creative*: imaginative construction of meaning, arts or performance.
4. *Using*: how to practise, manipulate, behave, engage in processes or systems.
5. *Higher-order learning*: advanced thinking, reasoning, metacognition.
6. *Dispositions*: attitudes, perceptions, motivations.
7. *Membership, inclusion, self-worth*: affinity towards or readiness to contribute to the group where learning takes place (James and Brown 2005:10–11, cited in Daugherty, Black, Ecclestone, James and Newton 2008).

We see that only the first two of these objectives deal squarely with the *content* of learning. The remaining five are about independent creative activity, metacognition and attitudes, which are outcomes we might all relate to personal development. These categories suggest that successful learning is as much about becoming a better learner as it is about mastering specific content.

5.1.1 The CEFR's model of learning

Section 4.2 introduced the CEFR's action-oriented approach, which identifies both general competences and specific communicative language competences. It is particularly instructive to review how the general competences are defined (section 2.1.1 in Council of Europe 2001). We have presented them in that section, and repeat them here in a little more detail:

- *knowledge*, i.e. declarative knowledge (*savoir*): all human communication depends on a shared knowledge of the world
- *skills and know-how* (*savoir-faire*): these depend more on the ability to carry out procedures than on declarative knowledge
- *existential competence* (*savoir-être*): the individual characteristics, personality traits and attitudes which concern self-image, one's view of others and willingness to engage with other people in social interaction
- *ability to learn* (*savoir apprendre*): mobilises existential competence, declarative knowledge and skills, and draws on various types of competence. It may also be conceived as 'knowing how, or being disposed, to discover "otherness" – whether the other is another language, another culture, other people or new areas of knowledge' (Council of Europe 2001:12).

The CEFR stresses that whilst the notion of ability to learn is of general application, it is particularly relevant to language learning; also ability to learn mobilises a range of other skills, such that 'attitudes and personality factors greatly affect not only the language users'/learners' roles in communicative acts but also their ability to learn' (Council of Europe 2001:106).

The Council of Europe Languages Policy Division, who gave us the CEFR, have a long-standing programme to instil the concept of *intercultural competence* in European education, with the goal of bringing up a Europe of tolerant and understanding citizens. They have expressed disappointment at the use of the CEFR in this respect, pointing to an 'obvious imbalance in implementation of the CEFR's provisions' which 'chiefly affects plurilingual and intercultural education, although this is one of the CEFR's main emphases' (Council of Europe 2010:5). Interestingly, the Council of Europe treats intercultural competence as something distinct from language education: they state that 'attitudes and behaviour, knowledge and skills relevant in intercultural contexts are *not* acquired as a side effect of developing language competences' (Council of Europe 2002, emphasis added). Jones (2016) counters that the Learning Oriented Assessment classroom fosters all the essential skills, dispositions and attitudes necessary to develop such competence. Surely, one outcome of becoming a good language learner is to develop an affinity with the culture where the language is spoken – that would certainly be the social constructivist viewpoint.

5.1.2 Learning and personal development

The above discussion leads us to see the important learning outcomes as less about mastery of content, more about changing the person and imparting new life skills: becoming a lifelong learner, a member of a learning community and a member of a broad society. In this view, positive dispositions, attitudes and images of self are at the centre, so that learning and personal development seem to merge into one and the same process.

Bereiter and Scardamalia (no date) endorse the view of learning as personal development in a critical appraisal of the constructs of what are called *higher-order* or *21st century* skills, such as *learning to learn, critical thinking, communication skills*, or *creativity*. On critical thinking they state:

> For good or ill, meeting the 21st century's need for good thinkers is being treated by education systems around the world as a skill-learning problem rather than a human development problem ... Although in the present climate it is heretical to suggest it, schools might be better off dropping thinking skills objectives altogether and turning instead to the time-honored goal of helping students develop as thinking persons (Bereiter and Scardamalia no date:17, 19).

We must clarify our use in this volume of the term 'skills', because the term is used very differently in first language and second language contexts.

In the context of L2 learning the term is used to identify competences which have value in society. It collocates easily with adjectives like 'practical', 'social' or 'professional'. The competences identified above in the CEFR's action-oriented model of learning might equally be described as skills. We commonly refer to speaking, writing, reading and listening as 'the four skills'. As illustrated in more detail in section 5.2, the models of language competence used in Cambridge English assessments reflect our best understanding of how language competence develops through social interaction to serve social purposes – the socio-cognitive model. The social constructivist learning paradigm adopted in this volume places social interaction at the heart of learning. In the second language context 'skills' are understood as the higher-order, emergent outcomes of learning.

This is very different from how the term is used in first language teaching. Thus Ivanič (2004) offers a framework of 'discourses' on teaching L1 literacy, ordered from a focus on the written text up to a focus on purpose-driven communication. Here 'skills' figure as the lowest level, reflecting a 'belief that writing consists of applying knowledge of a set of linguistic patterns and rules for sound-symbol relationships and sentence construction'. Above it come creativity, process, genre, social practices, and sociopolitical discourse. Ivanič places the terms 'purposeful communication' and 'higher-order communicative language teaching' at level 5, social practices.

The reason for this difference is obvious: in L1 for most pupils the language as a system is already effectively mastered, so that all discourses are potentially available, and to focus on the low-level mechanics of written text is to ignore or assume all the higher-level ones. Thus 'skills' refer to the basic understanding of sound–symbol relationships etc. upon which higher levels are based.

Bereiter and Scardamalia (no date) criticise the concept of '21st-century skills' precisely because using the term *skills* encourages a view of these as lower-level mechanical competences that can be formally trained, implying a reductionist approach to teaching them. Far better, they insist, to speak of personal development. This is coherent with the presentation of *emergence* in section 3.3.5, which treats communicative language proficiency as a *higher-order* skill.

5.2 The nature of language proficiency: Construct definition

Before we can teach 'language proficiency', or test it, or justify its importance to society, we must agree on what we mean by it. That is, we must define a specific *construct*: a theory or model of what knowing a language entails.

In the case of languages the CEFR's socio-cognitive model of language use and learning, introduced in section 4.2, provides a good starting point. The paragraph cited there describes a learner's cognitive apparatus (general knowledge, language competences, strategies), developing through engagement with communicative tasks that arise in social interaction.

Construct definition is a critically important process in which curriculum planners, teachers and assessment professionals ought to seek explicit agreement. To that list of stakeholders we should add society at large, because the purpose of education is to develop skills which will be useful and valued in society. Without such agreement it is quite possible that curriculum planners, teachers and testers will differ in their practice, and what is taught may not be the same as what is tested, or what is going to be valued in society, for example, in the workplace.

This seems too obvious to need stating, and yet research has indicated that weak construct definition is a common source of problems, so that in a range of contexts 'a diverse array of expertise, interest groups and government agencies dabble in the specification and assessment of learning outcomes, thus contributing to incoherence and exacerbating the alignment/congruence problem' (Daugherty et al 2008:247). The 'alignment/congruence problem' referred to concerns the alignment of teaching, assessment and social expectations to a shared conception of what a given school subject actually entails. The Study on Comparability of Language Testing in Europe, undertaken by Cambridge English for the European Commission in 2015, specifically addressed such issues. The European Parliament had suggested that existing national language tests might be used in place of expensive international surveys as a basis for evaluating learning outcomes. The results of the study (European Commission 2015) certainly revealed the problem of comparability when there is no consensus on construct definition or on other determining features of tests.

Where assessments are developed in a particular context then all stakeholders ideally should be involved in the process of construct definition. However, in the case of international exams like those provided by Cambridge English, construct definition falls within the domain of the assessment specialists: adopting the exams involves adopting the constructs of language proficiency which the exams implement.

In this case it is important that users of the exams understand and appreciate the constructs, and are ready to make whatever changes are necessary to learning materials and to teaching practice in order to prepare students for the exams. Thus if the exam is well chosen it will have positive washback on classroom teaching and learning; if the exam is a bad one the opposite will happen. The importance of construct definition in models of washback and impact is discussed by Green (2007), Hawkey (2006) and Saville (2009). The model of Learning Oriented Assessment presented in this volume seeks coherence between external exams and classroom teaching with the aim of achieving better learning outcomes.

Defining constructs to support the development of appropriate test tasks over a wide range of proficiency levels requires a lot of detail – considerably more, for example, than is provided by the CEFR, whose Can Do scales are essentially illustrative descriptions. This is particularly so in respect of models of cognition (Weir 2005a). Figure 5.1 offers a concrete example of construct definition, in the form of a model for reading.

At the centre of Figure 5.1 is the cognitive processing core, which begins with the low-level process of word recognition and works up to the highest level of comprehension. This cognitive processing calls on knowledge – of lexicon, syntax, the world, and conventions of writing. The reader also has a choice of strategies which determine how a particular reading task might best be addressed. On the assumption that for most readers learning constitutes a progression from lower to higher processes, the figure illustrates how tasks appropriate to a given level of reading ability might be specified and constructed.

This model is based on relevant theory, and supported by corpora of observed performance data. It is descriptive of how we believe cognition engages with reading, not prescriptive of how we believe it ought to. It is not a construct in the sense of a model arbitrarily constructed, but it is explicit about the posited cognitive processes, strategies and knowledge, and thus provides a good basis for setting item writers to work to construct test items which will be appropriate to a particular level of reading skill, the validity of which can later be defended. Figure 5.1 demonstrates how test tasks can be placed on a proficiency scale, enabling learners' performance on the tasks to be interpreted in relation to that scale.

Four volumes in the Studies in Language Testing series (SiLT) offer detailed analyses of the skills constructs as defined in Cambridge English

Figure 5.1 Illustration of a construct (Khalifa and Weir 2009:43)

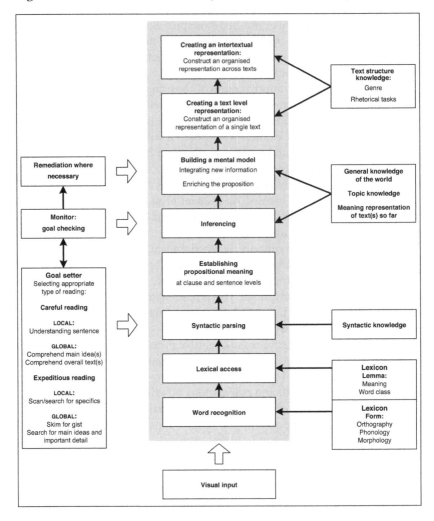

exams over a range of CEFR levels: Shaw and Weir (2007) for writing, Khalifa and Weir (2009) for reading, Taylor (Ed) (2011) for speaking and Geranpayeh and Taylor (Eds) (2013) for listening. Organised around Weir's validity model, these volumes set out to supply the useful level of detail which the descriptor scales of the CEFR itself do not.

In focusing language education on communicative language proficiency the concern is to ensure that the skills learned can be put to good use in society. That does not mean, of course, viewing communication in narrow utilitarian, instrumental or phrasebook terms, although there may have been a period, in the UK at least, where the novel concept of communicative language learning perhaps tended to be interpreted in just this way. Those involved in tertiary-level programmes still blame secondary education for 'dumbing down' language study.

As a social constructivist perspective confirms, communication is at the heart of the human condition, in the here-and-now and over time: Shakespeare continues to communicate with us across four centuries, and the generation of learners growing up in the age of social media are finding new but still language-mediated ways of communicating and sharing their experience of the world. The natural desire to communicate is a powerful force for learning if it can only be harnessed.

5.3 The content of learning: Curricular objectives

As stated above, curricular objectives and classroom practice must align with external assessment, and this means they must share a common understanding of the constructs that will be tested. Constructs define *skills* or *competences* – the *higher-order* outcomes of learning (see section 3.5). Curricula should identify these higher-order outcomes, but in practice will contain much more detail about the *inputs* to learning rather than the intended *outcomes*. They concern the *content* of learning, and how this is to be presented and sequenced over the course. They define what teachers have to do in order to bring about the desired higher-order outcomes, perhaps down to the level of the individual lesson.

There are of course a number of standard ways in which a curriculum can be organised: based on grammar, lexical frequency, communicative tasks, or a combination of these. Whatever the principle, there are several possible criteria for sequencing units of learning. One might start from what is most immediately useful, has greatest coverage, is easiest, simplest, most frequently encountered, the most appropriate to an age group, or to the specific needs of a group, and so on. Progression may be defined for general or for very specific learning contexts.

In a natural acquisition context, of course, there is no organised sequence, and yet learning still happens perfectly well. Organisation in a formally-defined curriculum is as much a logistical necessity as a question of optimising learning. Yet given that formal learning requires organisation it is still worth looking for help in identifying sequences which are somehow more effective than others.

For languages a number of tools are now available to curriculum designers, including the CEFR itself, and the range of resources which have grown up around it. Thus the descriptor scales of the CEFR help to identify expected progressions, for example in the qualitative aspects of spoken language:

range, accuracy, fluency, interaction and coherence, as outlined in Table 3 of the CEFR (Council of Europe 2001:28–29).

English Profile (www.englishprofile.org) has provided vocabulary and grammar profiles identifying the empirical sequences in which particular lexical or grammatical features are found to occur, given the evidence from very large learner corpora. A fairly reasonable assumption is that a curriculum which takes note of these is more likely to work well than one which ignores them. Such aids may help us to identify when a learner is ready to learn some feature, and are presented in explicit terms in documents such as the European Language Portfolio, which invite learners to exercise their metacognition in rating their own progress.

Approaches to organisation and sequencing will place more or less emphasis on the formal systems which they reference, and thus on the relative roles of cognition and metacognition in learning. Ideally we should think of two parallel outcomes to working with curricular objectives: a learning outcome, involving objective, metacognitive understanding, and an acquisition outcome, involving the cognitive development of higher-order communicative skills. Although a learning outcome may concern a single element of grammar or vocabulary, an acquisition outcome almost certainly involves assimilating a cluster of elements of grammar, vocabulary and other language that together lead to the mastery of higher-order communication skills. The nature of this longitudinal process of internalised acquisition of structures is most probably not linear or fully predictable, so that procedures for assessing the two kinds of outcome, and conceptions of mastery, necessarily differ.

5.4 In summary

This chapter has focused on the organisation of language learning within formal education, and discussed three aspects of the question: what is to be learned?

- the socially desired outcomes of learning
- the socio-cognitive *construct* of language proficiency (the *skills* to be acquired)
- the setting of curricular objectives (the *content* of learning).

The desired outcome of language study is, of course, that students learn to communicate in the language and have benefit of that. However, the social constructivist view makes us aware that achieving this outcome may be predicated on a prior outcome: a transformation of the learner's dispositions, attitudes and practical learning skills.

We are talking about *bringing out* the person, which is 'education' in the most literal meaning of the word – the 'time-honored goal of helping students develop as thinking persons', as Bereiter and Scardamalia (no date) state.

We saw that the term 'skills' is used quite differently in first language and second language contexts: for first language 'skills' are entry-level mechanical operations, such as spelling. For second language, the term relates to the socially valued higher-order competences that emerge as the result of successful learning.

The second aspect of the question 'what is to be learned?' concerns the constructs which define or describe language skills. Construct definitions should unite curricula, teaching, testing and society at large, so that the purposes of language education are shared and coherently pursued. Assessment boards might well be the best guardians of the construct, if they have the specific expertise to turn construct models into valid test tasks, and interpret performance on these in terms of levels of expertise, such as the CEFR levels.

Finally, we considered the relationship between higher-order communicative language skills and the objectives of learning as captured in curricular objectives. The notion of emergence allows us to understand that mastery of curricular objectives does not translate simply into communicative language proficiency; but we acknowledge that both are important.

6 The role of large-scale assessment in learning

> 'Were all instructors to realize that the quality of mental process, not the production of correct answers, is the measure of educative growth something hardly less than a revolution in teaching would be worked.'
>
> *Democracy and Education* (John Dewey 1916:183)

This chapter focuses on large-scale assessment as practised by examination bodies such as Cambridge English. The two key qualities of an assessment – validity and reliability – are introduced, and related to the specific requirement of Learning Oriented Assessment – that is, to promote better learning outcomes.

Clearly, success in learning relates to achieving the higher-order outcomes of learning identified in Chapter 5. A final school-leaving assessment must focus above all on that. But learning is a *process* as much as an outcome, and continuous, ongoing evaluation is part of that process: a shared responsibility of both teachers and learners. This is the essence of Learning Oriented Assessment as conducted in the classroom.

We have depicted these two levels of assessment as separate dimensions: one focused on measuring and interpreting learning gains, and the second focused on making learning happen for each student in the classroom. In this chapter we begin to bring these two dimensions together. Despite their differences they nonetheless share the same basic process: they are centred on *tasks*, which produce *language activity*, in conditions enabling *observation*, and learning. These conditions include an appropriate level of *challenge*, *comprehensible input*, and *scaffolding* which makes the task accessible. *Feedback* is generated, enabling performance to be *evaluated*.

This basic activity is adapted to particular purposes. Large-scale assessment requires more standardised control of contextual conditions, and formalised procedures for scoring performance. The feedback provided is more standardised and backward looking. In the classroom, on the other hand, feedback is immediate, forward looking, and more individualised.

These two dimensions of assessment produce different kinds of *evidence*, complementary to each other but both contributing to the dual purposes of assessment as defined here: to produce better learning outcomes, as well as better measurement and interpretation of those outcomes.

This chapter presents large-scale language testing as practised by Cambridge English. Chapter 7 will then consider classroom-based learning-oriented assessment.

Chapter 1 provided a first sketch of the systemic approach which is developed in this text, and explained why it is necessary to reject the now outdated dichotomy implied by the terms *summative* and *formative*. This clears the way to locating assessment within a coherent system, defining useful goals, providing evidence of progress towards their achievement, and accrediting outcomes in ways which make clear exactly what has been achieved, and which have wide currency.

Learning Oriented Assessment encompasses this wider, integrated system. In this chapter we will consider the requirements of large-scale assessments that ensure their validity and usefulness. There is a certain amount of technical exposition in this chapter, but the quality of assessment is not solely a technical matter; as Broadfoot and Black (2004:8) state: 'educational assessment must be understood as a social practice, an art as much as a science, a humanistic project with all the challenges this implies.'

6.1 Proficiency testing: The importance of criterion reference

Our focus is on testing language proficiency, rather than achievement. We wish firstly to identify where students are in their learning, on a path from beginner to advanced, and secondly to describe what it means to be there. Those two stages are critically important. The first concerns measurement, locating learners on a scale with a degree of accuracy; and the second concerns interpretation, which requires that we measure the right things, and that we have an understanding of what it means to be at a certain point on the scale (*construct definition*, as illustrated in section 5.2). Achievement tests relate more to *prescribing* a specific set of learning objectives – a syllabus or a course – and determining how learners have progressed in relation to these.

The proficiency/achievement distinction parallels the distinction between treating language as a skill or as a body of knowledge. Evaluating learning in relation to desired, real-world outcomes is called *criterion reference*. Evaluating learning by how learners rank in relation to each other – better or worse – is called *norm reference*.

In educational testing the proficiency and achievement aspects inevitably overlap to an extent; however, the distinction remains an important one, because ideally proficiency testing should help to maintain the focus on learning's higher-order objectives (communicative language proficiency) rather than an arbitrary list of curriculum content. Yet much depends on how proficiency is actually defined and measured, that is, the approaches to construct definition and to test design.

It seems common sense that we should focus on the useful outcomes of learning – that is, take a criterion-referenced approach to interpretation. However, education systems frequently fail to do so. Asset Languages, presented more fully in section 9.3, was a major educational project undertaken by Cambridge English which illustrates the tensions between proficiency and achievement testing in an English educational context, and the problems to be addressed in seeking a new, ecologically sound engagement with institutional language education.

6.2 Scale construction

Valid measurement begins with the construction of a common scale to which every individual test result can subsequently be linked. A candidate's proficiency, as found by their location on the scale, can be meaningfully interpreted, thanks to the way the test tasks have been developed to implement the language proficiency construct. A key aim for large-scale assessment is to standardise judgements or measures so that they remain the same across exam sessions. Subjective judgements are involved in marking the performance skills of writing or speaking (see section 6.5). Where measurement is based on candidates' objective scores, as is the case with tests of reading or listening, standardisation requires a statistical approach, which is the subject of this section.

The term 'scale' might be used for any kind of description of a progression from less to more: quantitative, qualitative, or a combination of both. Clearly, the most useful scales are those that combine effectively the quantitative and qualitative: accurate measurement and meaningful interpretation. This should be the major goal of scale construction. We will introduce the Rasch model, a statistical model based on Item Response Theory (IRT), also referred to as Latent Trait Theory (LTT). It is the scaling model used operationally by Cambridge. Scale construction is based on data – primarily, the responses of candidates to test tasks. It applies to objectively marked tests, which primarily means tests of listening and reading. The presentation below is adapted from Jones (2014).

Let us first consider the conception of measurement which IRT embodies. The metaphor of 'measurement' suggests that language proficiency can be measured just like physical attributes such as weight, length or temperature. But with mental constructs like 'language proficiency' things are not that simple. Objective measurement requires us to reduce the complex differences between people to points on a scale, defining a *trait* on which learners may rank lower or higher. A useful trait identifies a pattern in data which is strong enough to stand out from the individual variation. We also need a good qualitative or theoretical grasp of what we wish to measure in order to validate the quantitative findings.

The metaphor of measurement is not to be taken too literally. It suggests that language proficiency is something real in a person's head which can be quantified, like their height or weight, a view which does not fit with our current socio-cultural understanding of human abilities. Secondly, it implies that language proficiency, like temperature, has a unique meaning, as if a single language test could measure all learners in all contexts. However, every context of learning must be treated on its own terms. In other words, unlike temperature or length, measurement of language ability must begin with construct definition: what do we mean by language ability in the specific context for which the test is developed?

All approaches to testing which involve ranking learners by their score count as trait based: this is the familiar norm in school examinations and similar assessments. The major problem is with assessments that do not use an appropriate psychometric approach to measurement, so that the results are difficult to interpret meaningfully. The following section outlines the concepts underlying IRT and how they are put to work in an *item banking* approach to assessment.

6.3 Item Response Theory

First let us consider the shortcomings of 'classical' test statistics, which are the ones we are all familiar with from school: they include *facility*, the mean score on a test, the *pass mark*, and the *pass rate*. These are easy enough to understand: as more people score more than the pass mark, so more of them will pass the test. But these statistics have no unique meaning because they are all defined relative to each other: for example, if a group of learners scores badly in a test is this because the learners are less able, or the test is more difficult? That is not a question that can be answered neatly within classical test theory. To solve the problem it is necessary to think rather of the factors which underlie the scores we observe: the *ability* of test takers, the *difficulty* of test items and the *standard* which is applied. These are the absolute, meaningful values that we are really interested in: for example, a standard can be set in terms of a CEFR level, which can be given a specific interpretation.

IRT allows us to estimate and work with these absolute, meaningful values. Cambridge uses the Rasch model, which belongs to a class of models within IRT (Bond and Fox 2001, Hambleton, Swaminathan and Rogers 1991, Wright and Stone 1979). It exploits the fact that the *probability* of a learner responding correctly to an item depends on the *difference* between the item's difficulty and the learner's ability on a proficiency scale. The relation defined by the model is quite intuitive: when the person is relatively higher on the scale than the item she is more likely than not to get it right, and when she is relatively lower she is more likely to get it wrong.

Constructing a scale starts from test data – the correct and incorrect responses given by a group of people to a group of items. This implies a pretesting stage in development. Clearly, the higher the total score of each person, the higher their ability, and the higher the total score on each item, the lower its difficulty. That provides enough information to estimate the *proba-bilities* of any person responding to any item, and from this, the most likely values for all the abilities and difficulties, something that dedicated statistical software can do.

Finding the difficulty of test items is called *calibration*, and it is vital that all items in the bank are calibrated to the same scale. This is done by setting an arbitrary point on the scale at the beginning of scale construction and ensuring that every subsequent data set can be linked to it, by including some items which have already been calibrated. This is called *anchoring*.

In thinking about measurement scales it is important to keep separate in our minds the *measure*, and the *thing measured*, which reflects cognitive attributes of the learner, as elicited by content attributes of the tasks. Of course, our focus in testing is on the learners, but the test tasks constitute the lens through which we must view them.

As 'proficiency' is defined in terms of a measure, and interpretations of the measure, it therefore does not exist until someone measures it. We must distinguish this concept from terms identifying various kinds of ability or competence which are used in *defining* the construct of what is tested (such as 'grammatical', 'sociolinguistic' or 'strategic' competence). These describe properties of learners which are posited to exist in greater or lesser amounts, whether they are measured or not.

The argument for the validity of proficiency measures eventually comes back to our theoretical model of cognition – the *construct*, as illustrated in section 5.2 – and the interactions with test tasks that we predict we will observe, given the features designed into them (that is, we can state why we expect items to be harder or easier). To the extent that test performance empirically confirms these predictions then our claim for the validity of the test is strengthened.

6.4 Item banking

Item banking is a methodology for constructing tests and interpreting test outcomes using an IRT model. Its great value is that it creates an interpretive framework that encompasses exams at different levels, over different exam administrations and test versions, making it possible to generate tests with very similar measurement characteristics and to grade them to constant standards. Figure 6.1 gives a schematic view of item banking as a methodology for test construction.

Figure 6.1 shows on the left an item bank containing tasks ready for use in a test. The difficulty of the items in each task is known, that is, they have been calibrated. The data to calibrate these tasks has come from some form of pre-testing, and they have been calibrated to a single scale by using anchor tests, administered to pretest candidates together with the pretests themselves.

Figure 6.1 Item banking approach to scale construction and use (adapted from Jones and Saville 2007)

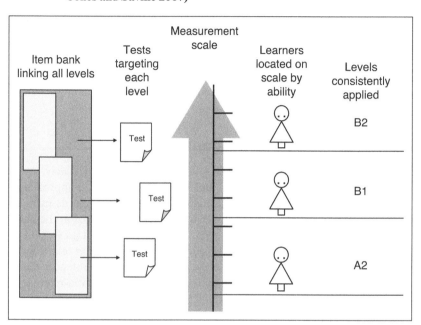

With the item bank stocked, tests are assembled by selecting tasks of appropriate difficulty for the target levels. Candidates' scores on tests locate them on the measurement scale according to their ability. Figure 6.1 shows tests at three levels, and three candidates. Although they might all have the same score – say, 70% – we know that 70% on the easiest test indicates a lower ability than 70% on the hardest test: knowing the item difficulties enables us to locate the candidates precisely on the measurement scale.

Finally, the standards are applied. These are fixed points on the scale which can be directly applied to establish each candidate's grade. Even if test versions differ slightly in difficulty, the standard can be held constant. Modifying the standard will impact all future tests in the same way.

Figure 6.1 thus illustrates the power of a fully functional item banking system. In such a system *ad hoc* standard setting is neither necessary nor possible. The great benefit of an item banking approach is not simply that it facilitates the construction of a stable measurement scale, but that in consequence it facilitates the construction of *meanings* which explain what it is that the scale measures.

Firstly, the items in the bank provide a concrete, detailed description of progression in terms of test content. Secondly, the fact that standards can be precisely maintained from session to session and from level to level facilitates doing the research to develop stable interpretations of learners' performance in the world beyond the test – for example in Can Do statements such as those used in the descriptive scales of the CEFR.

Thirdly, standards may be described in linguistic terms. English Profile (www.englishprofile.org) is a large-scale study which has produced a linguistic description of CEFR levels, identifying salient features of each level based on an extensive corpus of learner performance data (Hawkins and Filipović 2012). All such developments exploit and contribute to the meanings embodied in the measurement scale.

6.5 Performance assessment

The above description of how reading and listening are objectively tested using IRT shows it to be a technical and somewhat specialised approach to standardisation. However, the approach taken by large-scale assessment towards the performance skills of speaking and writing (at least in the practice of Cambridge English) is more recognisable as a standardised version of activities that also take place in the classroom. Standardisation relates both to judgements of performance and to the nature of the performances themselves. Judgements are standardised by basing them on criterion-referenced exemplars, and by rating schemes which reflect as explicitly as possible the construct of speaking or writing at the targeted level. Performance tends to be standardised through adherence to closely specified tasks, with the intention of making judgements more reliable; something which may be criticised from a social constructivist perspective (Leung and Lewkowicz 2006). Training and monitoring of raters is an essential aspect of ensuring validity and reliability, and the statistical apparatus of IRT can also be applied to standardising raters' performance by transparently compensating for the differences in severity which always exist.

The scales developed to support standardised subjective judgements of writing or speaking are essentially descriptive. There are two basic approaches: an analytic approach where different features are identified and separately judged (e.g. Range, Accuracy, Fluency, Interaction or Coherence); and a synthetic approach in which a single best-fit judgement is made, perhaps based on the same kinds of criteria.

In the classroom or the real world the impression of a learner's overall proficiency level is undoubtedly based primarily on the performance skills – precisely because they are directly apprehended productive skills – rather than the indirectly apprehended receptive skills of reading and listening. This suggests that the performance skills are a more relevant, practical and meaningful target for aligning judgements of level across classroom and large-scale assessments, something to which we will return later.

6.6 Validity and reliability of large-scale assessment

Validity is the key quality of an assessment system, and for Learning Oriented Assessment it must refer to both large-scale and classroom assessment, and to its fundamental purpose of producing better learning.

Various terms are used to describe the required properties of large-scale assessment. For example, Cambridge English identifies five concepts: *Validity*, *Reliability*, *Impact*, *Practicality* and *Quality*, where the last of these relates to the policies, processes and procedures put in place to ensure that the first four qualities can be achieved on a regular basis and to a high standard (Cambridge English 2013). Such process-oriented schemes reflect a change: from focusing on *validity*, seen as an innate property of a test, to *validation*, seen as the practical set of steps test providers can take to develop tests and defend their use for particular purposes.

However, *validity* and *reliability* remain two basic indices of assessment quality, and it is their reconceptualisation that is demanded by those who wish to do justice to the unique features of classroom assessment (e.g. Brookhart 2003, Moss 2003).

The notion of validity has evolved over the years, and current treatments have moved on significantly from the simple requirement to demonstrate that a test measures what it purports to measure. The modern understanding is reflected in Messick's (1989) definition of validity as 'an overall evaluative judgment of the degree to which evidence and theoretical rationales support the adequacy and appropriateness of interpretations and actions based on test scores'. This notion – that the validity of an assessment lies in *how it is used*, rather than in its intrinsic properties – represents an extension of (rather than an alternative to) the simple definition: a test cannot be used to positive effect if it is not in the first place well constructed and appropriate to the use in question.

Leung and Lewkowicz (2006:223) acknowledge that 'the expanded notion of validity . . . highlights the social value implications of test score interpretations and the social consequences of using test scores in education and other social contexts'. Rea-Dickens (2007:512) states further that:

> The traditional positivist position on language testing with the tendency to map the standard psychometric criteria of reliability and validity onto the classroom assessment procedures has been called into question, and the scope of validity has been significantly broadened and taken further by a number of researchers.

Thus this heterogeneous and socially oriented conception of validity would appear on the face of it to be potentially applicable to the specific context of

CBA, and sensitive enough to the requirement that all levels of assessment impact positively on learning.

The problem lies more in how validity is seen to relate to the second concept: reliability. Harlen (2005:247) asserts that 'it is well recognized that the concepts of reliability and validity are not independent of each other in practice. The relationship is usually expressed in a way that makes reliability the prior requirement.'

Reliability in assessment means something rather different to its everyday use, where it is commonly synonymous with 'trustworthy' or 'accurate'. As Feldt and Brennan (1989:106) point out, 'in everyday conversation, "reliability" refers to a concept much closer to the measurement concept of validity', that is, it implies that a test gives a 'correct' result. However, reliability in testing has the narrower meaning of 'consistent', in that a test should produce the same result on repeated use, and would rank-order a group of test takers in the same way. But this does not exclude the possibility that what it measures might be quite different to what it claims to measure, or what we would wish to measure.

It is true that validity and reliability have frequently been viewed as in conflict. Thus Spolsky (1995:5) identifies 'two major ideologies' underlying testing: a traditional British style relying typically on essays, and an American style relying on multiple-choice tests:

> To oversimplify, with the traditional examination we think we know what we are assessing, but remain happily or unhappily uncertain about the accuracy or replicability of our assessment; with the modern examination, we are sure enough of our measurement, but are, or should be, uncertain as to what exactly we have measured.

That is, tests can be either reliable or valid but not both. But this is something of a caricature. In trait-based approaches validity and reliability may actually be seen as closely linked, as both relate to the idea of measuring one thing at a time, using items that demonstrate high *internal consistency* – a feature also commonly used as a convenient proxy for reliability (Jones 2012). The nature and quality of the measure depends on the definition and implementation of the construct.

Reliability may indeed be prioritised over validity, as claimed by Harlen, if we boost internal consistency artificially by selecting items without due consideration for the construct, for example by using a narrow range of item types, such as multiple choice, or by omitting certain aspects of the skills or knowledge to be tested simply because they are harder to assess reliably.

For languages, in practice, testing the four skills separately produces measures, each of which fit a trait model well enough for practical purposes. The four-skills approach allows us to measure these complex aspects of communicative language proficiency without destroying the very thing we wish to measure.

We can also go beyond the trait model to extend conceptions of reliability. Mislevy (1994, 2004) evokes a broader conception of reliability based on the more complex evidence that newer forms of assessment may provide: 'this is not "reliability" in the sense of accumulating *collaborating* evidence, as in classical test theory, but in the sense of *converging* evidence – accumulating evidence of different types that support the same inference' (Mislevy 1994:8). This describes very well how Learning Oriented Assessment will need to deal with the complex evidence from classroom as well as large-scale assessments.

The nature of convergent evidence is also illustrated in Figure 6.2, which shows Weir's (2005b) socio-cognitive validity framework.

Figure 6.2 A socio-cognitive framework (adapted from Weir 2005b)

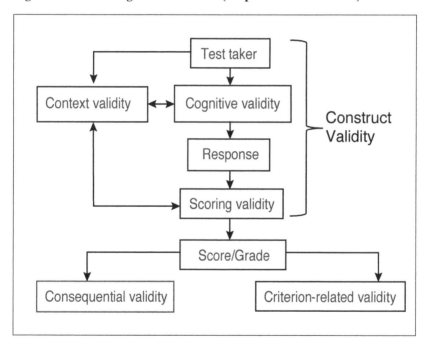

This framework is coherent with that of Messick (1989, 1996), and particularly useful for an exam provider in that it maps to steps in the test design and administration process, each of which impacts on validity, and which must therefore be a focus of attention. Figure 6.2 presents this framework in outline, showing the interconnectedness of the modelled elements. The test taker performs on test tasks which should have *context validity*, being relevant to the goals of the particular learner; and *cognitive validity*, meaning that they engage the learner's cognition in an authentic way. *Scoring validity* requires that the scoring mechanisms capture the learner's ability correctly. *Construct validity* relates to how all these elements interact to produce a valid measure.

Further elements within Weir's socio-cognitive framework include *criterion-related validity* which relates to how points on the measurement scale can be interpreted as indicating abilities or performance levels defined in real-world terms; and *consequential validity*, which relates to whether the impact of the exam is positive for individual test takers or society more widely.

6.7 Large-scale assessment: Evidence of and for learning

Large-scale assessment as presented above has significant potential strengths. It focuses on proficiency, enabling criterion-referenced interpretation of what has been learned, and consequently discouraging norm-referenced ranking of students. Thus it reports in terms which are positive for all students, both higher and lower performing. It is construct based, meaning that the nature of what is learned and how it relates to ability in a 'real world' is explicitly stated, and can inform the construction of both classroom and test materials. It uses a strong measurement model which ensures that scores on different test versions remain comparable and interpretable in the same frame of reference. Separate testing of the skills of reading, writing, listening and speaking goes some way to identifying individual profiles of language competence which can be reported. Even 'teaching to the test' should not be a problem, because the best form of exam preparation is to learn the language in question.

These should be crucial factors in defining how a school subject is conceived and taught, ensuring that the focus remains on useful learning outcomes, and discouraging subversion by extraneous purposes such as accountability testing. Additionally, summative assessment can also serve to support learning – in at least three ways according to Bennett (2011). First, citing Shepard (2006): if the content, format and design of the test offer a sufficiently rich domain representation, preparing for the summative test can be a valuable learning experience. Second, citing Rohrer and Pashler (2010), research suggests that taking a test can both enhance learning by strengthening the representation of information retrieved during the test and also slow the rate of forgetting. Thirdly, summative assessment may support learning by providing a limited type of formative information, to the extent that it is informative about a learner's profile of skills, and the opportunity exists to feed this back into further learning.

We could add a further distinct way in which summative assessment can support learning – by providing a motivating framework for setting, monitoring and pursuing learning objectives. For example, the Cambridge English suite of exams now covers all levels of the CEFR and thus constitutes a ladder of objectives that learners can (and some do) follow from the lowest to highest level.

Good summative assessment can thus provide evidence both *of* learning and *for* learning. Moreover, the evidence provided by such assessment is strongly complementary to that which can be collected in the classroom, as presented in the following chapter.

6.8 In summary

Let us summarise this chapter in terms of the two critical features of an assessment: its *validity* and *reliability*.

The validity of large-scale assessment begins with construct definition: an explicit model of how a language skill develops from lower to higher levels. Test tasks are written based on the construct definition. Tasks are then calibrated through pretesting, using an IRT model, and placed on a measurement scale according to their difficulty. In purely measurement terms, the validity of large-scale assessment hinges on whether the actual difficulty of test tasks agrees with their difficulty as predicted by the construct model. That would tend to validate our model of progression in learning.

In the context of Learning Oriented Assessment validity must also satisfy the extended concept where validity is evidenced by positive social consequences of using the assessment. For Learning Oriented Assessment that means producing significantly better and more useful learning outcomes. Reasons why large-scale assessment as described in this chapter might indeed show positive impact on learning outcomes include:

- focusing learners and teachers on higher-level outcomes (communicative language proficiency), making for better learning, and ensuring that test preparation provides an authentic learning experience
- providing a limited amount of formative information (achievement testing could play a role here)
- motivating learners by providing clear evidence of learning.

An obstacle to exploiting large-scale assessment to promote learning is its usual positioning as a summative event at the end of a learning process, when it is too late to make a difference. Forms of large-scale assessment which could contribute evidence of learning during rather than at the end of the process might well have far greater impact, although as the Asset Languages project demonstrated, serious logistic issues would need to be addressed.

Concerning reliability, it was noted that reliability and validity have been seen as in conflict with each other, with reliability generally winning out over validity; something which has doubtless been true in much school assessment, but need not be. Large-scale assessment as we have described it can achieve high levels of reliability without compromising on validity.

The challenge for Learning Oriented Assessment is to address Mislevy's conception of a broader conception of reliability (1994), based on combining a range of evidence including from classrooms: *converging* evidence that supports the same inferences.

7 Learning-oriented assessment in the classroom

'Give the pupils something to do, not something to learn and the doing is of such a nature as to demand thinking; learning naturally results.'
Democracy and Education (John Dewey 1916:160)

This chapter presents the two major concerns of the learning-oriented classroom: to generate interactions which lead to learning, and to capture evidence of interaction, in ways that maximise the impact on further learning.

7.1 The nature of classroom learning-oriented assessment

Understanding the nature of classroom learning interaction is important for evaluating any implementation of learning-oriented assessment: if it produces learning, we need to know *why* and *how*. This is Bennett's (2011:20) reason for insisting that 'formative assessment *is* assessment, at least in part' (see section 8.4).

Ideally we should limit the scope of what we include in the concept of learning-oriented assessment, to allow us to focus on its essential elements. In fact, we have explicitly identified social constructivism as the model of learning at the heart of Learning Oriented Assessment, partly for its particular relevance to the case of languages. Thus any learning improvement must be at least partly attributable to general social constructivist ideas.

Let us recall that our use of the term 'assessment' intends a much wider range of classroom activities than tests or quizzes. It refers to a focus of activity in the classroom on meaningful interaction, which will lead to learning, and the development of new psychological functions (see section 3.1). This is a form of assessment because it implements the assessment cycle of *performance–observation–interpretation–feedback*, with the primary purpose of promoting learning. Both student–teacher and student–student interactions may constitute a series of assessment cycles that produce learning: where classroom interaction is motivated by learners' purposeful use of language to communicate personally significant meanings, language acquisition processes are enabled which mirror to an extent those involved in learning a first language (see section 4.3).

In the classroom the assessment cycle operates over different periods. Wiliam (2006:7) identifies three such periods (see Table 7.1); we have particularly stressed the importance of the short-cycle interactions which help to scaffold students' performance, as does Wiliam:

> Basically, if you're not using information to make a difference to your teaching within a day or two then it's unlikely to make a difference to student achievement. It's the short cycle formative assessment that really matters, minute by minute, and day by day.

Table 7.1 Formative assessment cycles (adapted from Wiliam 2006)

Type	Focus	Length
Long–cycle	Across marking periods, semesters, years	4 weeks to 1 year or more
Medium–cycle	Within and between teaching units	1 to 4 weeks
Short–cycle	Within and between lessons	5 seconds to 2 days

We have suggested that students and teachers have specific responsibilities for learning. The onus on students is to develop the skills which will make them autonomous learners: the capacity to assess themselves and each other, and the appropriate motivation (see section 3.4.1).

Teachers have several roles, perhaps including formal assessment, but their central task is to create an environment conducive to learning, while sharing responsibility for the organisation of learning with students (see section 3.4.2).

If the above aspects of Learning Oriented Assessment may be seen as more general factors in classroom learning, what is more specific to it is the systemic linking of large-scale assessment to classroom assessment through a structure of *evidence* designed to feed back into better learning, and to align understanding of learning outcomes across the 'four worlds' of education, assessment, society and the individual. Learning Oriented Assessment coheres with the definition of formative impact by Wiliam (2006):

> What makes an assessment formative, therefore, is not the length of the feedback loop, nor where it takes place, nor who carries it out, nor even who responds. The crucial feature is that evidence is evoked, interpreted in terms of learning needs, and used to make adjustments to better meet those learning needs.

7.2 Domain-specific and generalisable learning skills

In our understanding of social constructivism learning may be seen as a process of personal development (see section 5.1.2), involving changes to learners' attitudes, dispositions and affinities, which impact on their learning skills (the CEFR's *savoir-faire, savoir-être* and *savoir apprendre* presented in section 5.1.1).

We would certainly be interested to know whether the development of learning skills is an intrinsic feature of the socio-cognitive model within Learning Oriented Assessment. If it were a demonstrable outcome of Learning Oriented Assessment this would certainly strengthen the case for its validity; but explicit testing of such skills would also carry risks, to which we return later (see section 8.4.2).

As discussed in Chapter 5 (in particular section 5.1), there are grounds for treating the components of *learning how to learn* as transferable, domain-independent skills. This is the position taken by Black and Wiliam (2009:23, see also section 2.3). However, others consider that learning-oriented assessment will be more effective if curriculum embedded (Bennett 2011, Shavelson 2008, Shepard 2006, 2008). 'Teaching for transfer' is a specific field of research which focuses on the transferability of skills across domains (e.g. Butterfield and Nelson 1989, Perkins and Salomon 1989). Its relevance to the case of language skills is not wholly obvious, it being cognitive constructivist rather than social constructivist in nature, based on laboratory experiments rather than classrooms, and focusing on the explicit teaching of transferable skills as algorithmic processes. The social constructivist view, and the concept of personal growth, seem to offer a plausible and more appropriate model of how learning skills can come to be transferable, through the personal development of the learner.

Thus we posit three types of learning outcome:

- domain-specific higher-order outcomes (the skill at the heart of the domain, for example, communicative language proficiency)
- mastery of domain-specific curricular content (for example, specific grammar or vocabulary which contribute to the emergence of the higher-order skill)
- domain-independent, transferable learning skills and dispositions.

7.3 Learning-centred and content-centred activities

A further defining feature of Learning Oriented Assessment may be its use of the concept of *emergence*, introduced in section 3.3.5, where we stressed its implications for pedagogy. If communicative language proficiency emerges as a higher-order skill which cannot be explained in terms of simple content transmission, then we cannot expect to achieve it in the classroom solely through a PPP (presentation, practice, performance) approach to teaching. Thus it is necessary to distinguish between *learner-centred* classroom activities, which promote emergence of the higher-order skills, and *content-centred* activities which focus on the assimilation of learning material as specified in the curriculum. Both require attention.

Learner-centred classroom activity enables learning to emerge from communicative interaction, between teacher and student, or student and student. By enabling learning through interaction and performance, the classroom takes on more features of an acquisition environment. Learner-centred activity highlights the Can Do interpretation of performance, criterion-referenced to levels on a proficiency scale, and thus orienting students and teachers on their progress. Thus classroom activity interpreted in the light of social constructivist ideas, and with a criterion-referenced focus on the individual learner, will prepare students better for proficiency-focused summative assessment than a purely content-centred approach.

Content-centred activity, on the other hand, is more coherent with a transmission model of learning. It focuses on the conscious learning and manipulation of linguistic forms, and the orientation it provides is more about the achievement of curricular objectives than performance in the real world.

We should emphasise the complementarity between these two aspects of classroom work: the emergence of higher-order skills in a classroom context doubtless requires scaffolding through the existence of a course structure and curricular objectives; the curricular objectives are more likely to be met and become part of the learner's competence when they are put to good use through the development of higher-order skills.

Specific approaches to teaching can also help bridge the gap between the two levels of learning, e.g. *focus on form* is a particular approach which links linguistic forms to the meanings that they can encode.

Thus the distinction between learner-centred and content-centred is a productive one for defining models of classroom learning interaction, and how this should link to more formal assessments. The relation is of theoretical and practical importance: how do they complement each other? How can we use the evidence they provide? These are issues to address later in modelling classroom practice and defining the big picture of learning-oriented assessment (see Chapter 8).

7.4 Classroom evidence *of* and *for* learning

The evidence from classroom-based learning complements that from large-scale assessment. It is used primarily by students and teachers, with the primary function of feeding back into further learning. Evidence collected within the classroom takes many forms and serves several functions:

- as immediate feedback to learners in the process of completing a learning-oriented assessment task
- for review by learners and teachers in evaluating the outcomes of a learning-oriented assessment task

- to monitor achievement against curricular course objectives
- to provide criterion-referenced interpretation of performance, e.g. in terms of CEFR level
- to recognise learners' achievements in more or less formal ways
- to motivate students
- to provide validation of Learning Oriented Assessment – does it work, and if so why and how?

Figure 7.1 reprises the schematic view of Learning Oriented Assessment in the classroom, which we first presented in Chapter 1.

Figure 7.1 The classroom within a Learning Oriented Assessment model

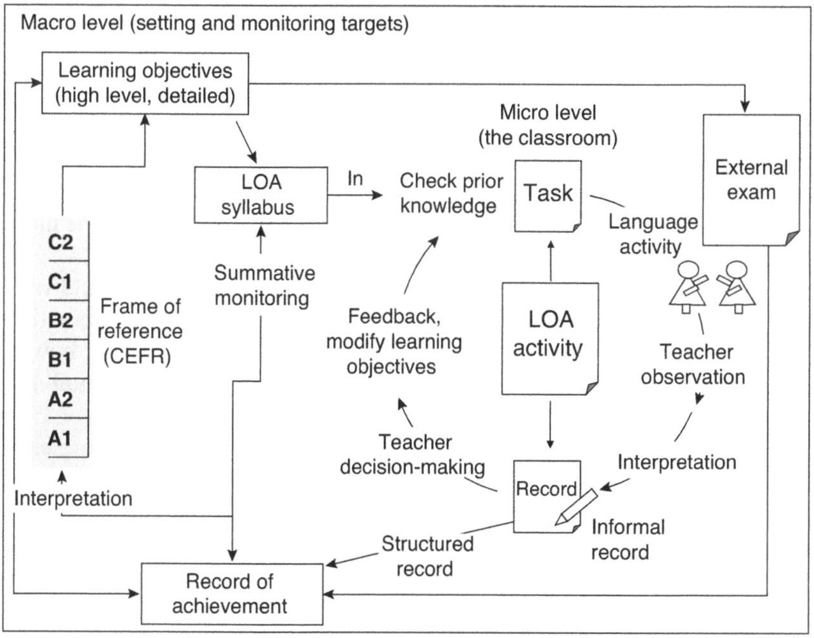

Figure 7.1 shows the assessment cycle of interaction, observation, evaluation and feedback, centred on a specific Learning Oriented Assessment activity. The Learning Oriented Assessment curriculum reflects higher-order objectives – that is, communicative language skills – and the specific content which will provide the input to this. This in turn is articulated within a frame of reference – in this illustration it is the CEFR – which locates the high-level objectives and specific content within a more widely shared conception of levels and learning goals. Within each assessment cycle a task is set which generates some interactive language activity. This is observed and interpreted

by the teacher, who perhaps makes some informal record. Feedback on the activity is provided by both teacher and students, and objectives are possibly modified – repeating, extending or additionally scaffolding the activity.

A structured record is also captured to maintain a record of achievement for each student. This can be interpreted within the CEFR frame of reference, and it also contributes to periodic summative monitoring of progress against higher-order objectives. At one or more stages in the course of study external exam results can also be contributed to the record – ideally not as a final summative judgement, but rather as feedback to guide further learning.

Acknowledging the importance of addressing specific curricular objectives, we identify a role for various measures of achievement. As Figure 7.1 illustrates, the record of achievement refers back to both the frame of reference (high-level goals) as well as to specific curricular objectives. What remains important is that simple feedback on achievement (such as a ranking of students by their marks on a test) should not detract from the significance of *qualitative* feedback from learning-oriented assessment in the classroom, or criterion-referenced interpretations of performance (for example in terms of CEFR levels). To the extent that external assessment remains strongly aligned with the higher-order goals of classroom learning-oriented assessment – that is, communicative language proficiency – learners and teachers will be more likely to focus on these.

Classroom interaction is where learning happens, and so we would wish to give due weight to the products and processes of classroom interaction – ensuring that it is observed, recorded, and evaluated. Whether, or how, it can be used to provide evidence of learning for high-stakes accountability purposes is a question we will return to below.

Evidence from the classroom may take a range of forms, capturing individual performances, but also, importantly, group interactions. Evidence may capture the *products* of classroom activities, such as completed exercises, pieces of writing, or audio and video productions; but also it should be possible with the support of technology to capture *processes*: such as the stages of a phased collaborative project. Validating learning-oriented approaches and progressively improving the learning value of classroom interaction will benefit greatly from such process-oriented evidence.

7.4.1 Evidence *for* learning

Providing evidence for learning in the classroom is about closing the feedback loop, so that students and teachers have the opportunity to reflect on, and perhaps repeat, extend and improve on, performance outcomes.

Evidence will be needed both of learner-centred activity and curriculum-centred work (see section 7.3), while taking care that the curriculum-focused record does not reduce to box-checking, and that the learner-centred record represents genuine instances of purposeful communication, rather than practised performances.

7.4.2 Evidence *of* learning

Evidence *of* learning serves important functions, for a range of stakeholders: governments use it to hold schools accountable; schools can use it to hold teachers accountable; or teachers themselves can use it to compare their performance against others. The pressure on the system which accountability testing exerts has been widely criticised (see section 2.2.1) but it remains a fact of life in many contexts. Above all, however, evidence of learning should feed back into the classroom to promote further learning: identifying problems to be addressed, or, more positively, demonstrating progress. For students, evidence of success in learning can be the best motivation for further learning.

Given the focus on higher-order learning outcomes, enough classroom time should be given to communicative activities, and this should produce records – written or recorded – available for later recall. Writing, as a collaborative or individual task, produces a permanent record which can be evaluated; the technology to keep good records of speaking activities is also readily available.

Criterion-referenced interpretation of performance, e.g. in terms of CEFR levels or learner-oriented Can Do statements, makes progress in learning visible, and keeps the focus on language use. Students should be enabled to judge their own and others' performance in speaking and writing: the option to compare against benchmarked exemplars of performance skills will be useful. Progress in the passive skills of reading and listening may be more difficult to make visible, but graded materials and tests made available by the external assessment provider might fulfil a useful role here.

External assessment, which could provide formal accreditation or certification, may be a 'big bang event' marking the conclusion of a student's whole school career, but in many contexts would function better as a graded 'ladder' of levels, providing a progression of motivating and accessible targets. This is what the Asset Languages project tried but failed to achieve (see section 9.3), as the additional costs and administrative overheads proved to be a discouraging factor for schools. Creating a multilevel testing framework which would be sufficiently light on administration and efficient in practice would be a challenge, but the benefits would be considerable, as it would enable effective individualisation of each student's learning path. As in so many areas, technology could play a role here by providing relatively lightweight assessments online. Such assessments would ideally have to provide feedback only to teachers, learners and parents; using them for accountability purposes would destroy their value.

The use of evidence of learning for accountability purposes remains an issue. We might wish to emphasise the role of evidence from the classroom, but any attempt to do this would have first to address the problem of standardisation. A significant advantage of using external assessment as the basis of judgement is that it is standardised: it provides a level playing field. Using evidence from the classroom might seem attractive, if it could give a more valid or detailed picture of what is being learned; but the standardisation issue is a real one.

One possible option is to look to the large-scale assessment provider to offer additional kinds of support for in-school assessment:

- to moderate and standardise the judgements of teachers, if these play a part in formal evaluation of students, or to provide exemplars of performance to enable schools to do their own standardisation
- to provide periodic or end-of-course summative assessment
- to provide curriculum-related diagnostic assessments
- to provide the comparative data to support wider (in-school, national, international) systems for monitoring performance.

The availability of such a range of services above and beyond the provision of external assessments may be an important issue to address in an implementation of Learning Oriented Assessment.

7.5 Learning-oriented assessment: An ecological model

The previous section began to illustrate how the evidence from large-scale external assessments and classroom-based learning-oriented assessment could be combined to produce optimal support for learning, within the range of sometimes conflicting purposes which assessment is made to serve in society. Here we develop this idea in more detail, considering the classroom and external assessment metaphorically as an ecosystem.

The social constructivist model of learning developed in this volume has made a number of assertions about the nature of learning:

- school learning proceeds within a community – it is a social process
- learning concerns personal development, consisting in attitudes, dispositions and skills which are key to present and future learning
- teaching goals and assessment goals must be closely aligned to specific desirable outcomes (communicative ability, in the case of languages)
- language learning concerns the purposeful use of language to communicate personally significant meanings
- tasks must have *interactional authenticity*, that is, learners must engage with the communicative task at hand, not on winning positive appraisal of performance

- evidence drawn from classroom interaction if systematically recorded could usefully be fed back to promote further learning.

Where these principles are successfully implemented then the classroom becomes an ecologically balanced environment, providing a school-based context that is conducive to learning and where there are no conflicting purposes. Protecting this environment is critical to learning.

Regard for the ecological perspective is necessary, given the evidence that in some contexts large-scale assessment does not work in the interests of better learning, and may indeed make for worse outcomes. Where assessment is a high-stakes issue for students, providing final accreditation of achievement at school, and even more so for teachers and principals, and where exam results are used for accountability purposes, there is an incentive to subvert the system by specific exam preparation – teaching to the test.

Such perverse incentives subvert examinations, and more critically, they subvert learning of the subject examined. To remedy this unhappy situation means dealing with the reality of the processes which may act to the detriment of learning. A successful system will be ecological in the sense that it will serve to advance socially valued outcomes rather than subvert them.

Let us consider Figure 7.1 as illustrating one possible model, where there are two distinct sources of evidence: internal evaluation, based on evidence from the processes and products of the classroom work, as captured in the record, and external evaluation based not on the classroom work, to which it has no operational access, but on a standardised exam credibly linked to the CEFR frame of reference.

Both the internal and external evaluations of achievement have a part to play: the internal evaluation, in addition to its fundamental role in classroom learning, has a monitoring function within the school, and can provide frequent feedback to teachers. The external evaluation happens in a longer timeframe, perhaps only once; so may not feed back into learning so directly. But it provides effective standardised, formal accreditation of achievements; additionally it offers a means of standardising (moderating) the judgements made at school level on the basis of the internal record.

This is one model of how different levels of assessment might be combined. In this model formal accreditation is based entirely on the external exam: no use is made of the classroom data. This might be deemed inappropriate in many contexts; but it has the important result that there is absolutely no danger of classroom learning-oriented assessment being subverted, nor of learners being coached to simulate proficiency rather than helped to acquire it, or to adopt performance goals over learning goals. If the significant benefits of adopting social constructivist, learner-centred, learning-oriented principles are to be realised, then insulating the classroom against subversion is vital.

There are, however, potential issues: the external exam is based on somewhat different kinds of performance (the skills of writing and speaking are less of a problem, but objective testing of reading and listening raises issues to be addressed), and it provides the standardised marks on which the school and students will be judged. Given these factors there is a strong incentive to focus on subverting the external assessment. But subversion can be prevented if two conditions can be satisfied:

- The skills constructs tested by the external assessment and the higher-order learning goals addressed in the learning-oriented classroom must be closely aligned. With this condition satisfied the best exam preparation is the learning-oriented classroom activity itself. This absolutely requires the adoption of a shared, construct-based conception of objectives (Daugherty et al 2008).
- The external assessment must be made robust against techniques of cheating, such as rehearsed performance.

To repeat: this is just one possible model. Other models might seek to maximise the information available for assessment by including evidence from both the external assessment and the internal record of learning-oriented class performance; but anything that requires classroom-based learning-oriented assessment to do double duty (Boud 2000) raises potential issues of subversion, at least in the accountability-driven cultures with which many of us are familiar.

There may be other contexts where the ecological solution might consist precisely in basing evaluation of outcomes on the classroom record, perhaps dispensing with any requirement for external evaluation. But this would require high levels of professional training for teachers, and begs questions about legitimate issues of standards and accountability.

The problems of subversion considered above are doubtless greatest where levels of learning outcome are lowest: a vicious circle of educational failure driving an accountability culture, which in turn drives further subversion of the goals of education. Relative failure in language education is evident in many countries, for whatever reason, as the ESLC (European Commission 2012) made clear.

Imagine the possible impact, in such an ailing system, of setting out instead to pursue the successful implementation of Learning Oriented Assessment. It might bring about very significant gains in achievement, turning the vicious circle of failure into a virtuous circle of success, and rendering issues of subversion irrelevant.

7.6 In summary

At the outset of this chapter we stressed the importance of understanding the nature of learning-oriented classroom interaction. If it produces learning, we need to know *why* and *how*. We have identified the following features of the learning-oriented classroom which should impact positively on learning:

- The nature of classroom interaction implements the assessment cycle of performance, observation, evaluation and feedback. Each of these stages can involve teacher–student or student–student interaction, and their goal is to understand and learn.
- The roles of student and teacher are well understood: students are equipped to manage their own learning, teachers are facilitators of learning interactions.
- Learning interactions are supported through scaffolding and appropriate choice of tasks, ensuring that progression is defined, and that each learner is appropriately supported.
- Use of language is meaning driven, achieving some of the benefits of an acquisition approach to learning.
- Nevertheless, acquisition can be supported by combining with certain activities e.g. focus on form.
- Engaging in classroom tasks thus has intrinsic motivation, making it more likely that students will be focused on learning rather than on winning positive appraisal. In other words, tasks have interactional authenticity.
- The nature of language proficiency as an emergent skill is recognised, so that adequate learning time is assigned to both learning-centred and content-centred work, and learning is not understood as a simple transfer of knowledge.
- Learning may be seen as personal development, and as such may lead to the development of generalisable learning skills.
- Curricular objectives may be defined and sequenced with reference to the same construct models which underlie the large-scale assessment; thus there should be coherence between the two levels of assessment, with benefits for learning.

A comprehensive validation programme for an implementation of Learning Oriented Assessment could begin with this list as a set of hypotheses to be explored.

In the second part of this chapter we considered possible forms of implementation of Learning Oriented Assessment, with evidence from external and internal sources being used in different ways. Depending on context there may be several ways of achieving an ecological solution – one where no element of the assessment framework is allowed to subvert the goals of learning.

8

Aligning large-scale and classroom assessment

'The two limits of every unit of thinking are a perplexed, troubled, or confused situation at the beginning, and a cleared up, unified, resolved situation at the close.'

How We Think (John Dewey 1933:106)

The two previous chapters discussed the evidence which large-scale assessment and classroom learning-oriented assessment can contribute to achieving the twin goals of better learning outcomes, and better measurement of those outcomes.

Bringing these different levels of assessment into alignment is the important final step, so that evidence from both levels can be interpreted within a common frame of reference. There are two aspects to this: firstly, to ensure that all levels of assessment focus on the same goals, and secondly that they report performance in terms of a common interpretive framework – that is, a common standard.

8.1 Alignment of goals

Alignment of goals is required in order to ensure that what is taught is what is tested, and that both serve purposes deemed to be of value to society.

This aspect requires a common understanding of what the goals are. In our presentation we have defined goals in terms of the *constructs* of the targeted higher-order skills (5.2 above). Pellegrino et al (2001) refer to alignment in terms of an 'underlying model of student learning', which sounds similar to our use of the term construct. Daugherty et al (2008) in their exploration of alignment in five educational contexts refer to *learning outcomes* as the target to which teaching and assessment should be aligned.

Daugherty et al's study shows how in practice problems for alignment arise in the articulation of targeted outcomes (given frequently inadequate construct definition) and how curriculum, teaching and assessment may diverge from these intentions (given issues of test-driven teaching and the use of assessments for accountability purposes). They conclude that alignment is not a simple notion, but is better understood as a 'complex, non-linear, interacting system' (Daugherty et al 2008:253).

In Gitomer and Duschl's (2007) terms, the issue here is one of *external coherence* with the concepts and socially valued learning outcomes of an education system. External coherence is an important concept, if we consider the evidence for how high-stakes summative testing has proved capable of undermining educational objectives in many contexts. It relates clearly to Messick's 1989 model of validity in assessment (see section 6.6), whose consequential aspects include the *values* which a test construct implies. It also recalls the metaphor of an ecological system, presented in the previous chapter.

8.2 Aligning interpretations of standards

The record of achievement which the student carries away from school may be based wholly on an external examination, wholly on judgements made within the school, or on some combination of the two. We cannot generalise across countries, although the Learning Oriented Assessment scenario that Cambridge English envisages is one where students will follow a course of studies, aiming to take a Cambridge English exam either as an additional qualification, or in place of a comparable school assessment. Whatever the situation, it is critical that all levels of assessment understand performance standards in the same way. Teachers should know roughly how well their students will perform in an external assessment. Students or their parents might wish to know what their grades in a school-based assessment are worth in terms of an international assessment standard. Generally, it is highly desirable that there should exist from the outset a descriptive framework which enables a shared understanding of each student's starting point, current level, and distance from their final goal – for example, articulated in terms of CEFR levels, and differentiated by skill. Such a 'learning landscape' is valuable in helping students to orient themselves in relation to their own progress, and to take ownership of their learning.

However, aligning standards in this way is not straightforward. In section 6.5 we acknowledged that the performance skills of writing and speaking are easier to deal with, because standardisation of judgements regarding such performance is similar across classroom and large-scale assessment contexts, being based finally on comparison with exemplar performances which are meaningful to teachers and learners alike, and which can be exploited within the classroom as useful aids to understanding and learning. In contrast, the indirectly observable skills of reading and listening are most readily assessed using objectively marked test tasks in an item banking model (see section 6.4): classroom versions of such tests might be provided to serve a progress-testing function, but these would not feed back so directly into learning.

Descriptive Can Do scales such as those of the CEFR are intended to help users to align their understanding of performance levels to a common standard, but their use is also not straightforward. Experience shows, for example from the ESLC (European Commission 2012:35), that such scales tend to norm themselves on expected performance levels in a given country or context: thus in a high-performing context CEFR statements are interpreted as describing a higher level, while a weakly performing country interprets them as describing a lower level. Thus teachers and students in a given classroom context will have no difficulty in ranking performances as better or worse, but may well be unable to link them correctly to the absolute performance levels intended by the CEFR. The external assessment body has an important potential role to play here in moderating judgements made at school or country level.

A further issue concerns *scaffolding*, and the comparability of observations of performances made in classrooms, in tests, or in the real world. The concept of scaffolding, as presented in section 3.3.2, is primarily thought of in relation to classroom interaction, where it describes the support given by an interlocutor (for example, a teacher) to bring a task within the capacity of the learner to engage with it. More generally it can be seen as a feature of all social interaction, where meanings are constantly negotiated, and also of classroom and large-scale assessments, where the performance elicited by a task may be scaffolded in various ways to bring it within the capacity to respond of a learner at the targeted level. One common form of scaffolding concerns the progression in a single unit of learning from receptive skills to performance skills: reading scaffolds listening, which scaffolds speaking, which scaffolds writing. Thus scaffolding is a ubiquitous feature of performance in tests, the classroom and the real world, and this makes it more difficult to align interpretations of such performance. It is also fundamental to learning, so that scaffolded performance is performance at the very growing point: as Fulcher (2010:75–77) points out, 'the whole purpose of "feedback" or "mediation" in CBA [classroom-based assessment] is to cause change'. We need ways to deal with this.

Simplest of these involves specifying certain performance conditions, for example: 'Learners can be said to have learned something if they are able to do something they could not do before *on demand*, *independently* and *well*' (paraphrased from Sadler 2007:390, italics in original).

Can Do statements intended to describe a task might attempt to be explicit as to the nature of scaffolding. Green (2012:155) proposes a synthetic approach to constructing Can Do statements with the following possible elements:

Activity: Can . . .	The social act (function) that the learner is to accomplish
Theme/Topic: Concerned with . . .	The themes, topics and settings in relation to which the learner might be expected to perform
Input text: Based on . . .	Nature of the text the learner might have to process as a basis for their own contribution

Output text: Producing . . .	Nature of the text the learner might be expected to produce
Qualities: How well?	For production these are grouped under the CEFR headings Linguistic, Pragmatic, Sociolinguistic and Strategic
Restrictions: Provided that . . .	Physical and social conditions in which the learner might be expected to perform

This is an ambitious attempt to factor in all the component aspects of task difficulty and how performance on the task might be scaffolded.

However, it remains difficult to create descriptions of performance which identify an absolute level. For example, take these two statements which sit adjacent to each other in a 13-level system of descriptors about dealing with 'general and curricular topics':

- understand some specific information and detail of short, supported talk on an increasing range of general and curricular topics
- understand most specific information and detail of supported, extended talk on a range of general and curricular topics.

Close analysis of these allows us to conclude that 'some specific information' is intended to be less demanding than 'most specific information', and that 'short talk' is less demanding than 'extended talk'; also, by inference, that there are probably other levels of performance which do not require detail, which are not supported, or require only a limited range of general and curricular topics, and so on. It would doubtless be quite easy to jumble the 13 descriptors and re-assemble them in the correct order; but it is hard to imagine that a single descriptor taken on its own could be used, for example, to uniquely identify a CEFR level.

Critical examination of such attempts at constructing Can Do statements to uniquely identify a level shows that it is barely practical, particularly using the word-processing approach illustrated above, where multiple versions of the same sentence are provided, modifying 'short' to 'extended', and so on.

This argument demonstrates the weakness of such an approach, but also points to a solution: human cognition is quite poor at making absolute judgements, e.g. of level, but it is excellent at making relative, comparative judgements of higher or lower, better or worse.

Therefore, approaches which exploit comparative human judgement are part of the solution to alignment. Comparative judgement (CJ) is currently an area of growing interest in the assessment world. In the UK a website called 'No More Marking' provides a CJ platform which makes this approach an effective and attractive alternative to traditional marking. Alignment of standards, for example across exam boards, is also something that CJ is well equipped to deal with. CJ exploits human judgement effectively by providing a strong psychometric framework for analysing the data which the procedure provides. For a fuller presentation of CJ see Jones (2014:40).

Other more complex psychometric approaches imply statistical modelling. For example, the difficulty of particular response formats in objectively-marked test tasks can be modelled and abstracted from the difficulty of the language point being tested. Thus Jones (1992) using data from an item bank of language-focused tasks was able to confirm a well-attested hierarchy of difficulty within a particular area of English grammar (Keenan and Comrie 1977), while showing that, predictably, a one-word gap-fill task type is systematically easier than a sentence-completion task type. Response format appears to be a generalisable difficulty parameter of objectively marked test items.

Thus, calibrating groups of related tasks within an IRT model can show up any progression in difficulty, and perhaps reveal the specific factors which account for difficulty.

A third approach is found in dynamic assessment techniques. Lantolf and Poehner (2011) describe an interventionist dynamic assessment procedure (see also section 2.4.2) whereby performance on a task is scored on the basis of how many clues or prompts the student requires in order to succeed on the task.

Thus scaffolding is a parameter which must somehow be accommodated in order to achieve comparability of interpretation of performances observed under differing conditions. This discussion has moved into technical issues which we shall not pursue here, but the issue has at least been raised.

In the previous paragraphs we have pointed out several issues to address in the alignment of levels of assessment, but we do not conclude from this that the goal of aligning teaching and assessment to shared, socially valuable outcomes is an unrealistic or in any sense meaningless one. The model proposed below provides an outline of how it may be achieved – at least for the case of languages.

8.3 Construct-based alignment of assessment

If communicative language ability may be treated as a skill with social and professional value, rather than a school subject with little intrinsic connection to use in the real world, then a clear basis can be identified for aligning teaching and assessment to desired outcomes, and thus to each other. Figure 1.2, presented in Chapter 1, depicted graphically the links between four intersecting 'worlds' of learning. It is reproduced in Figure 8.1 in slightly more detail, illustrating the roles performed within each of the worlds, and the factors which impact on learning.

The *personal world* centres on the *cognition* of the individual learner, and on personal factors which impact on learning: intrinsic motivation, autonomy, confidence, interest, experience, and so on.

The *social world* values learning outcomes which constitute useful *skills* – professional, interpersonal or existential. The world in which learning is rewarded, it provides extrinsic motivation, incentives, needs and opportunities, self-realisation, and so on.

The *world of education* sees learning in terms of *subjects* which can be defined through curricula and syllabuses, taught and tested. It implements a formal structure for learning, providing learners with experiences that are expected to promote learning. School subjects may or may not function as training in real-world skills.

The *world of assessment* is shown in Figure 8.1 as a separate world to that of formal education in order to underline the different, complementary roles which they should play in learning. This is a representation of how assessment would work within a Learning Oriented Assessment model, and not how it necessarily works at present. The assessment world sees learning in terms of constructs: models which link learner cognition to socially valued skills, and which allow development to be predicted, described and measured (see section 5.2).

Figure 8.1 Four worlds of learning revisited

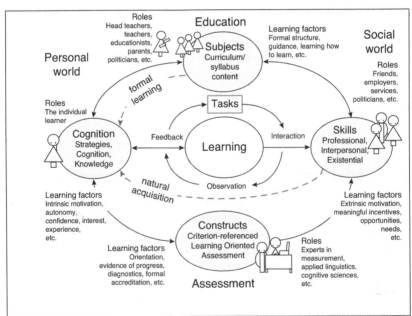

In this role assessment can provide learners and teachers with useful orientation, evidence of progress, and finally with valid formal accreditation of learning.

At the centre of Figure 8.1 is a generalised model of learning, and at the centre of that is the *task* (see section 3.3.1). All four worlds focus on tasks, although poor construct definition may lead stakeholders to interpret them differently (Daugherty et al 2008). In putting tasks at the centre of an approach to alignment it is essential that the constructs which the tasks implement and make observable are understood in the same way by schools, assessment bodies, governments and society at large.

The social world throws up wholly authentic tasks for individuals to perform, and much learning happens through engaging directly with such tasks (by the natural acquisition route indicated in the figure, as opposed to the formal route via the classroom). In the classroom, tasks may imitate the real world and are the focus of much interaction, enabling students' performance to be observed, evaluated and used to provide feedback into further learning. The assessment world also relies on standardised, construct-based and criterion-referenced implementations of tasks to elicit performances that can be evaluated and measured, and it is probably the assessment world which has ultimate responsibility for defining constructs, matching the nature of social interaction to the nature of the individual learner's cognition.

Thus the focus on skills naturally places tasks at the centre, as the construct which, exploiting the notion of *interactional authenticity* (see section 3.3.1), potentially enables comparison and alignment across domains – the classroom, the assessment and the social world. 'Potentially', because as discussed above there are differences in the way tasks are performed and evaluated in the different domains, and each individual's performance may require specific interpretation.

So far we have introduced the concepts of *external coherence* with a shared set of educational or social values, and *internal coherence* in terms of their demonstrable alignment within a common assessment system, including common understandings of specific criterion levels of achievement.

The notion of *task* seems relevant to both dimensions. It focuses on social action, placing a specific charge on education to teach language for socially important purposes: work, relationship with others, self-realisation in the world. This concerns *external* coherence. In relation to the development of learners' cognition it affirms the fundamental importance of communication as a means as well as an end of learning, and in terms of general models of learning it affirms the social constructivist view of learning as a shared activity which develops each individual's feeling of identity of purpose within the group. These points are relevant to internal coherence, as it should follow that task-based performance in classroom or assessment contexts will engage and impact on the learner's cognition in the same way, and can also be interpreted in terms of its likely effectiveness in society – that is, it links to the objectives of learning.

Figure 8.1 is not specifically a model for language learning. It should in principle be equally relevant to any subject taught in school, if we accept that there should be coherence between school subjects and skills valued within society (which need not, of course, be exclusively instrumental or utilitarian). However, there is currently much greater consensus that language should be taught as a useful skill, and consequently there is a solid framework in teaching and assessment practice that can be built on. This may be less evident in the case of other subject domains.

8.4 Evidence within a Learning Oriented Assessment model

Previously we have considered the kinds of complementary evidence which large-scale assessment and classroom learning-oriented assessment can contribute to achieving the two fundamental purposes of assessment: to describe and report outcomes of learning, and to bring about further learning – evidence *of* and *for* learning.

This is at heart a question of validity – the assurance that the evidence which an assessment furnishes is fit for the purposes it claims to serve. This is Bennett's (2011) intention when he states that:

> . . . formative assessment *is* assessment, at least in part. This fact implies that relevant measurement principles should figure centrally in its conceptualisation and instantiation. Incorporating measurement principles doesn't mean that validity should be sacrificed for reliability, as some advocates fear, or that inappropriate psychometric concepts, methods, or standards of rigour intended for other assessment purposes should be applied. But it does mean we should incorporate, rather than ignore, the relevant fundamental principles (Bennett 2011:20).

The 'relevant principles' are that the observations made, their interpretation, and the actions taken in consequence, should all be clearly defined and justified. The basic cycle of observation, interpretation and consequential action, which is common to all levels of assessment from the classroom to large-scale summative assessments, must be implemented in all contexts with sufficient care that the evidence provided is credible.

8.4.1 Proper uses of evidence

An important aspect in the ecology of an assessment system concerns how and by whom evidence is used. Hattie (2005) asks: what is the nature of evidence that makes a difference to learning? In an Australian/New Zealand context, he states that 'schools are awash with data, and the accountability movement is requesting that they collect even more' (Hattie 2005:11). What he presents is a system squarely focused on collecting data for accountability purposes, but with an interestingly different focus on the primary use of such data. Data on students' performance should be used in the first instance to assist teachers to judge their own effectiveness (relative to local or national benchmarks), although the model also permits other key stakeholders (principals, ministries, parents, students) to share this evidence. Hattie's simple concept of using feedback to teachers to drive up standards is presented within a more complex and coherent framework aimed at using data to help define the meaning of those standards, that is, the goals of learning: 'Outcomes from curricula must have a sense of *achievement progression* . . . One of the major purposes of an accountability system is to assist in articulating a common language of progression' (Hattie 2005:14).

Thus curriculum development should reflect evidence on what students know and can do, based on large-scale testing of items across the curriculum. From this, explicit definitions of learning intention, success criteria, and how these will be assessed can be provided to students, empowering them to self-regulate their learning by giving them evidence of learning performance.

Hattie's assertion that accountability testing properly conceived can function ecologically remains challenging, but his discussion of how data can best be used to impact positively on learning is valuable.

8.4.2 Evidence of ancillary effects

In the course of this text we have identified a set of important learning skills, attitudes and dispositions which learners may carry away into life after school. These emerged from the nature of learning in a social constructivist view, which seems to be better described in terms of personal development: changing the person, and in particular making them a better learner. We deferred the important issue of how, or whether, such skills should be assessed. We should find forms of evaluation which give due weight to these important educational outcomes; however, to give them due weight does not necessarily mean testing them explicitly.

These are ancillary skills, and may be better evaluated indirectly, by studying their impact on the development of primary skills (here, communicative language ability). We might use the metaphor of investments, which are evaluated by the interest they generate. The skills of learning pay interest in the form of better learning and self-efficacy: during schooling and then through a lifetime. We are familiar with the magic of compound interest: over time, the benefits accrue faster and faster.

It should be possible, then, to approach evaluation of these ancillary learning skills indirectly, through measuring the primary learning outcomes. Testing individual students is not the only way of judging educational outcomes, and carries its own dangers, given the negative impact of governments re-purposing test results (see section 2.2.1). In section 5.1.2 we cited Bereiter and Scardamalia's (no date) critical appraisal of treating so-called *thinking skills* as constructs to be explicitly taught and measured, rather than as outcomes of personal development through education. A European Commission project to develop an indicator for the skills of 'Learning to Learn' (Fredriksson and Hoskins 2007:251) also shows constructs being shaped by a focus on accountability and measurability: 'The political imperative to identify indicators . . . has brought about a situation . . . characterised as "the proverbial assessment tail wagging the curriculum dog"'. These examples warn us of the dangers of identifying such skills as explicit objectives of an educational system.

Thus evaluation of ancillary skills based on specific research, rather than testing of learners, may be the best approach to confirming their positive impact on learning. Section 9.6 gives an account of the kind of impact research which could effectively evaluate this category of learning outcome. This would be preferable to trying to measure and objectify skills and dispositions which cannot readily be measured or objectified without risking subversion of the very thing we wish to measure.

8.4.3 Can evidence be re-purposed?

Another issue concerning the proper use of evidence relates to how evidence collected in the classroom for formative purposes might be recycled for summative purposes. The ARG literature proposed that, for example: 'Teachers also need to be clear about the ways in which information gathered as part of teaching can be used formatively to help learning and then summarised and judged against reporting criteria for summative uses' (Harlen 2009).

As discussed earlier, the distinction between what Harlen calls *big* and *small* ideas, and which we distinguish as the emergent relationship of higher-order skills to lower-level learning objectives, makes such re-interpretation difficult. In fact, it is quite unreasonable to expect that a measure constructed from the results of lower-level observations (for example, classroom tests or exercises with a lexico-grammatical focus) should correlate highly with students' demonstration of higher-order communicative skills. We might also conclude that it is unnecessary, as what is finally tested and accredited should relate to the higher-order skills, or at least rank them significantly higher than the lower-level curriculum objectives.

8.4.4 Evidence of how students learn: Big data

This discussion of evidence has focused on learning in terms of how it changes the learner. A different perspective is to consider how evidence might deepen our understanding of the skill or competence itself. English Profile (www.englishprofile.org) is a large-scale study which has produced a linguistic description of CEFR levels, identifying salient features of each level based on an extensive corpus of learner performance data (Hawkins and Filipović 2012). Such approaches use *big data,* as such very large datasets are known, to discover regular patterns which would otherwise be impossible to detect, in order, for example, to model the behaviour and the learning trajectory of different groups of learners.

There are already many online learning environments which attempt in different ways to model learning, based on the availability of big data that records the interaction of learners with the system. Such systems use machine learning techniques to improve the way they interact with the learner.

Pellegrino et al's (2001) book *Knowing What Students Know: The Science and Design of Educational Assessment* explores how human teachers or intelligent systems might be able to use explicit models of cognitive processes to diagnose learners' individual states of understanding and help them progress. Such a programme is essentially an attempt to model in detail the states of knowing or partial knowing which are explored in the dialogic interaction between teacher and learner that is the locus of learning.

Evidence for learning based on big data is likely to become an increasingly significant field in the coming years.

8.5 The validity of Learning Oriented Assessment

It is too early to talk of validating the model of Learning Oriented Assessment presented in this volume, given that no fully comprehensive implementation has yet been attempted. However, it is possible to review the issues that need to be addressed in any implementation, and the evidence of validity which might be provided.

Turner (2012) reviews the emergence of CBA as a field of activity separate from high-stakes assessment, and requiring a different conceptualisation of the fundamental concepts of reliability and validity. In the belief that setting a new research agenda would be timely, she poses six questions, which we will answer below with reference to the arguments put forward in this volume. Turner's questions are shown slightly paraphrased below, together with our current best answers:

• *What are the quality criteria? How can reliability and validity be reconceptualised within a socio-cultural framework?*

We have identified a range of high-level outcomes of learning within a social constructivist approach: competence in the core subject, but also the *learning how to learn* skills and dispositions that should lead to significantly better learning both at school and throughout life (see Chapter 5). The validity of learning-oriented assessment will be demonstrated above all in these significantly better outcomes.

This requires that outcomes can be measured, implying the availability of well-designed and administered large-scale assessments. It is particularly important that these assessments function in an ecological manner, supporting the achievement of classroom learning objectives rather than subverting them. For classroom-based learning-oriented assessment to be effective it must be allowed to focus primarily on learning, and not be made to serve other functions which risk undermining its validity (see also section 7.5).

- *What are the characteristics of assessment tasks that provide a context for learning? What is the evidence for these bringing about change in learning?*

Interactional authenticity is key (see section 3.3.1). Tasks are contexts for purposeful interaction, not exercises to be completed. While curricular objectives will necessarily specify lower-level, detailed objectives, how these contribute to the emergence of higher-order communicative skills must be carefully considered. Approaches such as *focus on form* (see section 3.3.1) can help achieve the necessary articulation.

- *What is the nature of teacher/student feedback and reflection that influences the effort towards and outcome of further learning?*

To be effective this must be based on serious interaction within a group. A socio-cultural constructivist approach favours this. The roles of teacher and learner in the classroom may need radical adjustment (see section 3.4.2), giving learners more power to control their own learning.

- *What defines the role(s) and responsibilities of 'assessor'? How do teachers and students interpret their roles? What impacts on their decision-making?*

Peer-assessment and self-assessment are skills that will enable learners to take responsibility for their learning. Teachers must learn to share the role of assessor, and must focus equally on immediate goals and higher-order outcomes. How assessment and the provision of feedback is conducted, and how this impacts on learners' approach to learning, are important issues (see section 3.4.1). Above all, assessment must not be seen as a function outside learning, but rather as an integral aspect of the learning process.

- *How do teachers reconcile CBA and preparation for external tests? What are the commonalities needed to create coherence across these different assessment components?*

Such reconciliation of the goals of external and classroom-based learning-oriented assessment absolutely requires the adoption of a shared, construct-based conception of objectives (Daugherty et al 2008, see also section 9.1). A focus on tasks and interactional authenticity potentially provides the link between the four worlds of the learner, the school, society and assessment, although we have indicated issues of comparability across contexts, given that performance in all contexts is scaffolded in some way.

As stated above in addressing the first point, it is also essential that the distinct purposes of classroom-based learning-oriented assessment and large-scale external assessment be clearly identified, and classroom work stringently protected against subversion, e.g. in the way outcomes are directed towards accountability purposes.

- *How should pre-service and in-service teachers be supported so they can effectively engage in assessment that supports learning?*

To quote the title of James and Pedder (2006), we must go *beyond method*. Teachers should understand and be able to work from first principles in their approach to implementing learning-oriented assessment, be absolutely clear about the higher-order skills which make up the targeted outcomes, and be competent in linking curricular objectives to those outcomes. High-quality pre-service and in-service training is certainly essential, and clarity as to objectives must be shared across all levels: the literature reviewed in this volume repeatedly confirms the difficulty of successful implementation (see section 9.2), given the new and different demands placed on all participants in the learning process: learners, teachers, assessment bodies and educational institutions.

Our model of Learning-Oriented Assessment insists on the importance of a relatively small number of fundamental principles, though it will require a high level of expertise on the part of assessment bodies and teachers. We acknowledge the practical issues in implementation, but we believe that current recognition of the need to improve educational practice and outcomes, supported by the properly directed expertise of assessment bodies, can still be a powerful force for change.

9 Implementing Learning Oriented Assessment

'A problem well put is half solved.'
Logic: Theory of Inquiry (John Dewey 1938:108)

This chapter looks ahead to the issues to be addressed in the full-scale implementation of Learning Oriented Assessment.

It considers some of the concerns which motivate current policy-making with regard to educational goals in general or languages in particular. It reviews the literature on formative assessment for case studies to illustrate the practical difficulties, paying particular attention to the lessons of the Asset Languages project, which attempted but finally failed to provide an alternative assessment framework for languages in England. It looks to the role of technology in providing potentially game-changing support for all aspects of Learning Oriented Assessment. Finally it illustrates the conduct of *impact studies* in contexts where Cambridge English exams have been adopted within state or regional educational systems, with the consequent requirement to evaluate outcomes and identify issues.

9.1 Educational policy-making: The global scale

A relatively recent historical development in educational policy-making is the evolution of a supranational frame of reference, against which outcomes in particular countries may be compared. While this is evidence of governments showing a keen interest in the success of their education systems, it is not without issues.

Partly this development reflects the evolution of supra-governmental structures, such as the European Union, with the European Commission as its executive. Thus for example the European Commission (2012) identifies the further development of language competences as crucial to employability, mobility and growth, contributing to achievement of the objectives of the Europe 2020 strategy on growth and jobs (strictly, national education policy does not fall within the remit of the Commission, but growth and jobs do).

However, the global scale of the current educational frame of reference is above all an outcome of the development of a range of international educational surveys, including the Programme for International Student Assessment (PISA), Trends in International Mathematics and Science Study (TIMSS), Progress in International Reading Literacy Study (PIRLS), and Programme for the International Assessment of Adult Competencies (PIAAC). The ESLC (frequently referred to in this volume) is a recent addition, first administered in 2012 by the SurveyLang consortium, led by Cambridge English (European Commission 2012, Jones 2013).

International surveys provide at best a partial picture. Critics claim that the evidence they provide plays too dominant a part in determining how countries compare and evaluate themselves: surveys get too much attention, relative to other high-quality educational research (Alexander 2012, National Research Council 2003). At the heart of this concern is the tendency of policy-makers to interpret survey outcomes simplistically as a league table of better- or worse-performing countries, leading to possibly quite ill-judged responses. Policy-makers endorse the concept of *evidence-based policy*, but as previous discussion has shown (see sections 8.4 and 7.5), if the aim is to produce better learning then the scope and use of evidence must be much more broadly conceived than the simple headline outcomes of international surveys.

Certainly, there is evidence from research that as a way of 'driving up standards' the managerial conception of evidence-based policy is not effective. If we are to implement ecological models of Learning Oriented Assessment, including a role for standardised assessment of the kind practised by Cambridge English, then this is a crucial message to communicate to policy-makers.

At the same time, the ESLC produced findings which could readily be interpreted as consistent with the model of language learning proposed in this volume. Jones (2013:5) summarises thus:

> A language is learned better where motivation is high, where learners perceive it to be useful, and where it is indeed used outside school, for example in communicating over the internet, for watching TV, or travelling on holiday. Also, the more teachers and students use the language in class, the better it is learned.

This paragraph describes language being used for motivated, purposeful communication. However, the ESLC made clear that this ideal learning situation was approximated only in some countries, and effectively, only for English.

9.2 Worlds of difference: Predictable implementation issues

International educational surveys also remind us how greatly the context of education differs across countries: economic and developmental differences, different cultural perceptions of the purpose and nature of education, and even national stereotypes (press coverage of the ESLC showed that countries tended to use the results to confirm their image of themselves as 'good' or 'bad' at languages) – all these factors make clear that Learning Oriented Assessment will necessarily have to take into account the specific context of implementation. But at the same time we can learn from the history of formative assessment to identify predictable obstacles to successful implementation, and perhaps address these better. Black and Wiliam (1998a) offer three conclusions from the literature on teachers' assessment practices:

- formative assessment is not well understood by teachers and is weak in practice
- the context of national or local requirements for certification and accountability will exert a powerful influence on its practice
- its implementation calls for rather deep changes both in teachers' perceptions of their own role in relation to their students and in their classroom practice.

Many other authors identify the pitfalls of implementing learning-oriented assessment models in various contexts. Issues that successful implementations will have to address include the following.

- Policy-makers and politicians must be persuaded of the primary imperative of ensuring good classroom practice, and not subverting it by inappropriate use of learning outcomes for managerial and accountability purposes (Broadfoot 1996:39, Mansell et al 2009).
- At the same time there are dangers in governments reforming too much and too quickly. As Cumming (2009) and Davison and Leung (2009) point out, the adoption of criterion-referenced, communicative goals for language learning raises fundamental issues about how language proficiency is defined, how assessments should align to curricula, and how pedagogy should approach formative assessment. Such radical changes require a very high level of support.
- A general issue explored by Daugherty et al (2008:244, see also section 8.1) is that the constructs of interest – the desired goals of learning – are 'often strongly contested and expressed in a multiplicity of ways'. Achieving clarity of aims requires attention to construct definition (see section 5.2), to how progression is defined in curricula, to assessment procedures, and to misuse of assessment for accountability.
- Generally, summative models of assessment continue to dominate and shape forms of assessment even in contexts intended to be formative (Harlen and Malcolm 1996, Leung and Lewkowicz 2006).
- Teachers tend not to distinguish between formative and summative assessment and may even resist reforms that challenge their preference for summative assessment (Broadfoot and Black 2004).

- The term 'formative' may be interpreted as organised information gathering which informs the teacher but doesn't help students about how to make progress towards further learning (Assessment Reform Group 1999:7).

- Doing formative assessment well is extremely difficult and calls for high levels of teacher competence. Shepard (2000:12) is one of many writers to acknowledge this, noting that the social constructivist view of classroom assessment which she has presented is an idealisation: 'clearly, the abilities needed to implement a reformed vision of curriculum and classroom assessment are daunting.'

- In consequence, better teacher training is essential, and it must address the fact that teachers may be called to play a leading role in quite different kinds of assessment: classroom learning-oriented assessment, but also high-stakes summative testing (Brindley and Burrows (Eds) 2001, Cumming 2009, Murray (Ed) 2008, North 2000, Nunan 2007).

- Implementations may pay too little attention to the learner. While teachers need to be highly skilled in learning-oriented assessment, Davison and Leung (2009:399) point out that 'the learner's role is crucial because it is the learner who does the learning.'

- Finally, public attitudes and awareness may not favour implementation of learning-oriented models. Phelps (1998:16) summarises the results of a large-scale survey conducted in the USA: 'What about "teaching to the test" and "narrowing the curriculum"? It would appear that the public has strong opinions on both practices: they like them and they want them.' Hattie (2005:12), in an Australian context, observes that 'it is incorrect to blame the politicians. They are clearly listening to the voters – who want more accountability (which they interpret as tests and data)'.

9.3 Asset Languages: A cautionary tale

In 2002 a major study – the Nuffield Inquiry – led to the launch of a National Languages Strategy, initiating a bold reform to promote communicative ability as the primary goal of language education. Cambridge English was contracted to supply the assessment system called for by the National Languages Strategy. It was an ambitious project including summative and formative strands, and eventually encompassing all the levels of the CEFR and 25 languages. For a more detailed account of the Asset Languages scheme see Jones (2014).

In short, the scheme attracted a devoted but relatively small following, and finally it was wound up in 2013 after falling numbers of entries and changes in official accreditation policy made it unsustainable.

Finally, Asset Languages did not succeed in its attempt to re-focus attention on the purposeful use of language for communication. It proposed a different set of educational priorities, but was ultimately unsuccessful in communicating these new values to potential users – teachers and school heads. The fate of Asset Languages demonstrates that on its own a reforming assessment scheme cannot make a difference. A successful implementation of Learning Oriented Assessment will integrate coherently curriculum design, teaching practice and assessment of outcomes. Reform which does not encompass the whole system, or which does not communicate its values effectively, is unlikely to succeed.

9.4 Technology to the rescue?

Technology offers us ways of engineering a transformative shift of emphasis in how learning is conceived and implemented. It offers an opportunity to 'break out of the box' (the traditional classroom) and create a wider ecological environment to support effective language learning. We have presented Learning Oriented Assessment as an integrated system where classroom assessment and external large-scale assessment collaborate to contribute evidence both *of* and *for* learning. Evidence is the basic currency of Learning Oriented Assessment, and technology offers practical ways of generating and interpreting such evidence, and feeding it back into further learning.

As the John Dewey quotations at the head of each chapter have sought to illustrate, the key ideas of social constructivism and of Learning Oriented Assessment as developed in this text have been around for a long time, and have largely defeated the efforts of generations of educationists. If we believe that these are ideas whose time has finally come, this is down to, among other things, the technological support now potentially available.

Technology can now impact on every stage of learning interaction:

- *Delivery and mediation of assessment and learning tasks*: Chapelle (2009) considers how SLA theory might inform computer-based learning interactions, identifying a number of such learning theories within the fields of cognitive linguistics, psycholinguistics, general human learning theory, and language in social context. For example, VanPatten's *Input Processing* theory (VanPatten 2007) focuses on psycholinguistic mechanisms for making form–meaning mappings, and thus could inform the construction of instructional materials to exploit this theory.
- *Capturing and recording data*: A detailed record can be captured of individual and group performance on tasks, formative classroom interactions, students' own individual records of and reflections on their learning, both in and beyond the classroom.

- *Tracking progress against goals*: Achievement against curriculum goals and higher-order criterion-related performance can be monitored.

- *Individualisation of the learner's experience*: Students' performance can be interpreted and appropriate feedback provided instantly, orienting the learner with respect to successful learning as well as problem areas. Learning can be made more effective by tailoring tasks to particular features of learners: their overall proficiency level, specific issues relating to, for example, first language, possibly choice of topic, learning style, and so on.

- *Extending learners' experience of language beyond the classroom,* providing more authentic tasks and learning experiences.

- *Enabling new forms of learning interaction,* such as real-time or asynchronous communication, perhaps with students in a different country. Clearly, maximising engagement in authentic, meaningful communication is an essential element of the social constructivist classroom.

- *Improving our understanding of learning*: Computers can identify patterns in very large datasets and apply machine-learning techniques to progressively improve the algorithms that drive the interaction between the learner and the system. This may provide new insights into the nature of learning.

Creative thinking is needed in this area. Above all, evidence must be generated in the classroom, co-constructed with students and fed back into further learning: turning evidence into action is critical.

9.5 New contexts of learning

In the previous section we referred to the classroom as the locus of learning, and to classroom-based learning-oriented assessment as the interactive process which leads to learning. This will doubtless continue to reflect most contexts of learning which would be of interest; however, technology already supports a number of new approaches to learning, offering alternatives to the traditional classroom.

9.5.1 The flipped classroom

The flipped classroom is a pedagogical model in which the typical lecture and homework elements of a course are reversed. So far more commonly applied in higher education, the most typical format for the material to be studied at home is an online video recording of a lecture, perhaps even delivered by a heavyweight academic; the classroom activity involves the same or a different teacher, whose role is to animate and control a session of group-based work.

This enables students to exchange ideas and confirm and deepen their understanding of the material; the teacher's time is more productively spent in animating this process. With its aim of ensuring that classroom time is spent as far as possible on collaborative work, the flipped classroom clearly incorporates social constructivist principles.

9.5.2 MOOCs

A recent development in distance education (c.2012) is MOOCs: Massive Open Online Courses. A MOOC is an online course aimed at unlimited participation and open access via the web. MOOCs can deliver teaching through a range of traditional course materials such as videos and readings, but their most characteristic feature is the interactive user forums that bring together learners and teachers in a virtual learning community.

MOOCs share properties of the flipped classroom: learning material is presented largely in transmission mode, but the learning experience is enhanced through subsequent group discussions within a virtual learning community.

9.5.3 Adaptive learning

A substantial number of companies with backgrounds in information technology or in educational courseware are now offering adaptive learning systems which set out to individualise learning by catering to the specific needs or preferences of each learner. Such a system may be deployed with or without a role for a human teacher, although experience shows that some form of central direction is of benefit. The responsibility for directing learning might by negotiated between teacher, learner and the system. The adaptive system comprises a number of *models*:

1. The expert (or *construct*) model defines the underlying skills to be taught. Thus, it could describe progressively higher levels of performance in terms of the *tasks* and *performance levels* expected of learners at different levels.

2. The teacher (or *instructional*) model fulfils the role of teacher (unless there is a human teacher in a blended learning environment) and manages the form of *content presentation and development* within the adaptive learning environment.

3. The learner (or *student*) model builds a picture of the individual learner. The simplest interpretation of a learner's skill level is the method employed in computer-adaptive testing, which relates purely to an estimate of the learner's ability, based on the difficulty of the tasks which can be successfully completed (see the presentation of IRT in section 6.3). This allows learners to be directed to content at an appropriate level

of difficulty. A more sophisticated student model would deduce other features of the learner's style, such as their learning and forgetting rate, or preference for particular forms of presentation.

Adaptive learning is clearly relevant to the development of learning-oriented assessment theory and practice, and *vice versa*: the insights into the processes of learning developed in this volume feed naturally into work on the algorithms underlying adaptive learning. The capacity of the adaptive system to capture and analyse huge amounts of data can enable detection of subtle patterns in behaviour related to the interactions between the expert, teacher and learner models, which in turn should feed back into identifying optimal approaches to human-led classroom learning-oriented assessment.

9.6 Positive impact by design

The concept of Learning Oriented Assessment has grown out of studies of the impact of introducing Cambridge English exams into national education systems – a development which has become a significant area of research. The notion of positive impact starts from the premise that an assessment body has a duty to maximise the positive and minimise or eliminate negative impact, aiming at 'positive impact by design' (Saville 2009, 2012). Learning Oriented Assessment may be seen as a theory of action aimed at achieving positive impact by design.

The focus in this section thus moves from the evidence needed to implement Learning Oriented Assessment to the evidence needed to evaluate the impact of a given implementation. Impact can be studied in quantitative terms, such as measured levels of performance on tests, but qualitative evaluation is also critically important. It helps understand why and how learning is happening, at a number of levels, including most importantly the level of classroom interaction.

The Learning Oriented Assessment model aims at broadening the range of evidence collected in the classroom, exploiting a range of technologies to capture process data, such as records of groups working collaboratively. Primarily intended as feedback into learning, such rich data will also have a role to play in impact research, and research will equally feed back into improving classroom practice. Thus implementing Learning Oriented Assessment will logically entail aligning its theoretical framework and data model with that of impact research.

In the next sections we illustrate methodological approaches to the study of impact, as well as the issues which may emerge from such evaluation. Salamoura, Khalifa and Docherty (2014) present the background and development of the concept of positive impact, illustrating with two case studies, conducted in Vietnam (Khalifa, Nguyen and Walker 2012) and Spain (Ashton, Salamoura and Diaz 2012, Salamoura, Docherty and Hamilton

2013). The following section draws on that paper, and includes a summary of the first of these studies.

9.6.1 Studies of impact

Bachman was one of the first scholars to present impact as a quality of a test which should be integrated within the overarching concept of test usefulness (e.g. Bachman and Palmer 1996). In 1992 Cambridge English introduced impact as one of its four essential qualities for test development and validation: Validity, Reliability, Impact and Practicality, or *VRIP*.

Milanovic and Saville (1996) proposed an early model for achieving positive impact, focusing on the importance of working with stakeholders in a given context. It built on four maxims:

1. Plan
2. Support
3. Communicate
4. Monitor and evaluate.

Planning implies the development of testing systems and processes according to an explicit cyclical and iterative model. This requires regular reviews and revisions, allowing for improvements to be made when necessary (Cambridge English 2013:31–32, Saville 2003:57–120). *Support* concerns all stakeholders involved in learning and teaching towards internationally available examinations. *Communication* concerns engaging with stakeholders and providing an appropriate level of information (Cambridge English 2013:31–32). *Monitoring and evaluation* acknowledges the essential requirement to collect data on test performance and on the contextual features of particular groups of test takers. This involves routine analysis, as well as specific research programmes to investigate impact effectively. The discussion of *evidence* in this chapter makes clear the complexity of the data relevant both to achieving and identifying positive impact in the classroom.

Saville (2009) proposes a meta-framework for conducting impact research effectively under operational conditions. This enables anticipated positive impacts to be achieved more effectively, and the introduction of improvements to systems, as necessary. Positive impact starts with test design. It sets out to anticipate possible consequences of using a test in particular contexts (Saville 2009, 2010). Key concepts within this model include:

• *Test construct.* Impact by design builds on Messick's (1996:252) idea of achieving 'validity by design as a basis for washback'. As illustrated in section 5.2, test development and validation should be based on explicit definitions of the tested constructs. Adequate construct specification helps ensure that the test is fit for purpose and that its validity is not threatened by construct underrepresentation or construct irrelevant variance (Messick 1996:252).

- *Test delivery systems.* For the test to operate effectively in a given social and educational context the construct must be reflected in all teaching and learning preparatory to the test. This underlines the need for effective communication and collaboration with stakeholders, as noted in the Maxims 2 and 3, and discussed further in the Cambridge English *Principles of Good Practice*, Section 2 (Cambridge English 2013).

- *Context.* As illustrated in section 9.2, context is critical in investigating educational processes. Understanding the nature of context and the roles of stakeholders was an early priority for Cambridge (Taylor 2000). Education proceeds within complex systems with dynamic interplay between many sub-systems and 'cultures' so that understanding participant roles is critical to bringing about intended changes (e.g. Fullan 1993, 1999, Thelen and Smith 1994, Van Geert 2007). It is particularly important to understand the interplay between the macro and micro levels in a given context, and to determine elements which facilitate or hinder desired outcomes.

- *Timeline.* Understanding test impact in a new context requires a long-term validation plan, with consequences for the design and implementation of an impact study. Several phases may be involved, so that comparative data over time can be captured.

We should think of impact by design as more about *anticipation* than *prediction*. Possible impacts on both micro and macro levels can be anticipated as part of the design and development process, and where potentially negative consequences are anticipated, remedial actions or mitigations can be planned well in advance. See also Khalifa and Saville (2016).

9.6.2 Research methods

The epistemological principles underlying choice of research methods for evaluating test impact reflect the stance of *critical realism* (Sayer 1984, 2000), while theories of knowledge and learning are coherent with pragmatism, constructivism and a situated cognition perspective (see section 3.1.1). Impact by design is situated in 'real world' research paradigms which set out to determine 'what goes on' in contexts of test use (Robson 2002). Research is shaped bottom up – from individual perspectives to broader, more general understandings. The approach is participatory in nature, seeking collaboration with and involvement from various stakeholders.

Impact questions are particularly suited to mixed methods research (Creswell and Plano Clark 2011:69, Moeller, Creswell and Saville (Eds) 2016). Cambridge English has created an 'impact toolkit' of methods and approaches for carrying out analyses of both large-scale aggregated data, as well as micro analyses of views, attitudes and behaviours in local settings. Quantitative analysis of macro-level group data allows us to capture overall patterns and trends, while the qualitative analysis of multiple single cases enables researchers to monitor variability in local settings and to work with the 'ecological' features of context. The integration of both analyses provides an in-depth understanding of the data, offering insight and practical interpretation.

Finally it is important to highlight the composition of the impact research teams. Collaboration between the examination provider and local researchers is essential. It ensures capture of relevant data, deeper and more accurate understanding of the educational context, and insight into both macro- and micro-level contextual parameters. Many issues arising can only be resolved if a wide range of local stakeholders agree to jointly acceptable solutions; the challenge is to get the relevant stakeholders working together effectively.

9.6.3 Research questions

The studies reported by Ashton et al (2012) and Salamoura et al (2013) relate to the primary or primary/early secondary education context. They investigate the introduction of external assessments within local educational programmes introduced in state or state-subsidised schools, with the aim of improving English language learning outcomes. Research questions were the same for both studies:

1. What is the intended/unintended impact of the educational initiative?
2. What is the impact of the test/new initiative on key stakeholders, namely, teachers and learners?

Common constructs explored under these two questions include: attitudes towards teaching, learning and assessment; learner and teacher motivation; learner progression; teaching practice/development; parental involvement. Both studies used multiple data sources in a convergent parallel mixed methods research design (Creswell and Plano Clark 2011).

Instruments were selected from the Cambridge English 'impact toolkit' and adapted for the specific context where necessary using expert judgement prior to implementation. Quantitative instruments included surveys and test score data; qualitative instruments comprised interviews and, for young learners in particular, focus groups. Both studies were collaborations between Cambridge English and local researchers with an in-depth knowledge of the local context. See also Moeller, Creswell and Saville (Eds) (2016).

9.7 Steps in implementation

The case for Learning Oriented Assessment presented in this volume has been built from theory, or principles. We believe that a strong theoretical base is necessary for successful implementation. Figure 9.1 provides a final outline of the journey made in this volume: from theory to practice, and back again to theory.

Figure 9.1 Steps in implementation: From policy to evaluation of outcomes

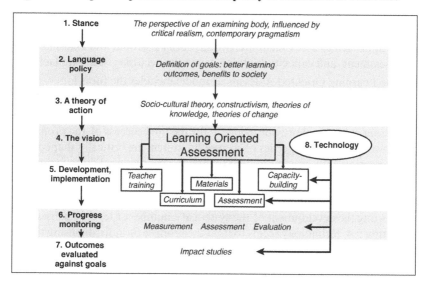

1. *Stance* is the perspective of the examining body: the set of principles which inform our approach to assessment.

2. *Language policy* is framed by governments, who may accept the assistance of the exam body if they share its goals and stance. Policy must have the scope and weight to produce the transformations in practice which may be necessary.

3. *A theory of action* seeks to ensure that implementation is coherent, consequential and rational. It will have several dimensions. At the level of the classroom we must go beyond method, equipping teachers (and learners) to understand and apply the socio-cultural, constructivist principles behind the method. More generally, the theory of action should draw on complexity science as applied to studying change in organisations (businesses, or schools). Saville (2009) states that:

> ... educational systems are complex and dynamic so that linear or causal relationships between planned changes and actual outcomes cannot be predicted with any certainty. The consequences – intended and unintended – emerge after the test has been "installed" into its real-life contexts of use ... From this perspective the overall validity of an assessment system is an emergent property resulting from a test interacting with contexts over time.

4. *Learning Oriented Assessment* is the name we have given to the comprehensive system which has better learning as its goal.

5. *Implementation* of this system will require a series of co-ordinated developments: teacher training, curriculum and materials development, an approach to assessment integrating both classroom and external assessment, and capacity-building where the necessary skills are lacking.

6. The Learning Oriented Assessment model includes the tools for *monitoring progress and giving feedback* that can be directed to bringing about further improvements.

7. *Impact studies* will provide evidence for the final success of the project. However, as the properties of a complex system are critically shaped in interaction with its environment (context), accurate prediction is not possible.

Figure 9.1 also finds a place for technology, shown as a facilitating resource supporting the development of the system at a number of levels. As discussed in section 9.4, technology seems to hold the promise of individualising teaching and learning, monitoring and supporting each learner's progress, and thus enabling significant gains.

9.8 A conclusion

Sceptical readers who have got this far may still feel that examination boards are the last people to whom the future of education should be entrusted. They can point to recent episodes such as the impact of the *No Child Left Behind* legislation in the United States, or to the 'perverse incentives' created by the use of school exam results for accountability purposes in the UK. They can cite governments' use of exams and testing to 'drive up standards', and its demonstrable failure to do any such thing.

They can point to Finland, which performs so highly on international surveys, and yet 'has no national tests, no league tables, no draconian national system of inspection, no national teaching strategies, and indeed none of the so-called "levers" of systemic reform in which the British government has invested so much' (Alexander 2012:12). Doubtless, educational assessment can be part of the problem, or part of the solution.

We can, of course, speak only for Cambridge English Language Assessment. In this volume we have introduced a model of Learning Oriented Assessment which seeks to put learning at the heart of assessment. It has not come out of nowhere: over the years the range of Cambridge English examinations has grown into a 'learning ladder' of objectives, covering all levels of competence, and well supported by textbook publishers, as well as through the wraparound services offered by Cambridge English itself. Learning Oriented Assessment is a response to the changing profile of the candidature, and particularly the adoption of the exams in compulsory education where English language is often an obligatory part of the curriculum from elementary school upwards, where there may be a need for closer engagement with teaching and learning, and more risk of adverse impact.

Implementing Learning Oriented Assessment is partly a question of re-purposing core assessment competences: the definition of constructs that explicitly link learning outcomes to the real world; the writing of tasks which embody those constructs; the use of criterion reference to offer learners a clear, meaningful picture of progress; and the capacity to measure that progress accurately. All of these have immediate relevance to the classroom.

What is new is the model for engagement with particular contexts of learning at all levels, from ministries down to the classroom. Every context differs: as the ESLC demonstrated, levels of language-learning achievement in European schools vary from very high (Sweden) to very disappointing (England), with every possible level in between. So even in Europe, there is a great deal to be done to improve language-learning outcomes. The CEFR offers an accessible, action-oriented model for language learning, but it is striking that many countries who make reference to the CEFR are failing to understand or implement its philosophy. A relatively simple adjustment towards learning-oriented assessment concepts might produce substantial gains.

If the potential of Learning Oriented Assessment is to be realised it will require co-ordinated changes at every level. Policy-makers must recognise the harm done to learning by using exam results for managerial purposes – a position predicated on mistrust and failure. There is a more attractive alternative: to allow exams to encourage higher achievement by focusing on valued learning outcomes, rather than on uninterpretable grades. If this can be done then learning the subject becomes the most effective form of exam preparation, predicated on trust and success.

In this volume we have linked classroom-based Learning Oriented Assessment to a small set of fundamental principles, including:

- the school is a community and learning is a social process
- learning concerns personal development of attitudes, dispositions and skills vital to present and future learning

- teaching and assessment goals must be closely aligned to specific desirable outcomes (communicative ability, in the case of languages)
- language learning involves the purposeful use of language to communicate personally significant meanings
- tasks must have *interactional authenticity*, that is, learners' cognition is engaged on the communicative task at hand, not on winning positive appraisal of performance
- evidence drawn from classroom interaction should be fed back to promote further learning, so must be systematically captured.

With these principles in place the classroom can focus on learning: there are no conflicting purposes. Protecting this environment is critical to learning. The above principles are not negotiable, even if we recognise that each context must be treated on its own terms, and that we must be prepared to deal with a long process of transition. Along with others who have discovered the difficulty of doing formative assessment well, we will doubtless find that implementing change is a long-term process. Teacher training will be a key aspect of any implementation. Technological support for the teacher in collecting and using evidence will be important. However, even if Learning Oriented Assessment implies mastering new methods, it is teachers' endorsement of the basic principles which will make the fundamental difference.

Teachers espousing these fundamental principles and supported by training and purpose-built Learning Oriented Assessment classroom materials and tools will, in turn, be empowered to:

- set both higher-order learning outcomes and more specific curricular objectives, acknowledge their complementary aims, and understand the necessity that these two ought to be aligned in terms of goals, constructs and frames of reference for learning to work
- identify the different types of assessment and their purposes
- use them to elicit complementary evidence *for* and *of* learning (e.g. from an informal classroom interaction which yields feedback on curricular objectives to large-scale assessment which links performance to higher-order learning goals)
- collect this evidence in a systematic way and make appropriate interpretations
- turn evidence into individualised learning by providing feedback and necessary scaffolding to help learners operate within their *zone of proximal development*
- ultimately, build learners' ability to learn, producing better learning and better outcomes.

In writing this volume we have focused on language education, but the most valuable gain in our own understanding which this study has provided is the realisation that the key skills which make good learners are transferable across subject disciplines. To state what should be obvious, but is too often forgotten: education is not about the transmission of content, but about changing the person, and equipping them to continue their development in the world beyond school.

Appendix 1
Assessment for learning: 10 principles (Assessment Reform Group 2002)

Principle 1: Assessment for learning should be part of effective planning of teaching and learning

A teacher's planning should provide opportunities for both learner and teacher to obtain and use information about progress towards learning goals. It also has to be flexible to respond to initial and emerging ideas and skills. Planning should include strategies to ensure that learners understand the goals they are pursuing and the criteria that will be applied in assessing their work. How learners will receive feedback, how they will take part in assessing their learning and how they will be helped to make further progress should also be planned.

Principle 2: Assessment for learning should focus on how students learn

The process of learning has to be in the minds of both student and teacher when assessment is planned and when the evidence is interpreted. Learners should become as aware of the 'how' of their learning as they are of the 'what'.

Principle 3: Assessment for learning should be recognised as central to classroom practice

Much of what teachers and learners do in classrooms can be described as assessment. That is, tasks and questions prompt learners to demonstrate their knowledge, understanding and skills. What learners say and do is then observed and interpreted, and judgements are made about how learning can be improved. These assessment processes are an essential part of everyday classroom practice and involve both teachers and learners in reflection, dialogue and decision-making.

Principle 4: Assessment for learning should be regarded as a key professional skill for teachers

Teachers require the professional knowledge and skills to: plan for assessment; observe learning; analyse and interpret evidence of learning; give feedback to learners and support learners in self-assessment. Teachers should be supported in developing these skills through initial and continuing professional development.

Principle 5: Assessment for learning should be sensitive and constructive because any assessment has an emotional impact

Teachers should be aware of the impact that comments, marks and grades can have on learners' confidence and enthusiasm and should be as constructive as possible in the feedback that they give. Comments which focus on the work rather than the person are more constructive for both learning and motivation.

Principle 6: Assessment should take account of the importance of learner motivation

Assessment that encourages learning fosters motivation by emphasising progress and achievement rather than failure. Comparison with others who have been more successful is unlikely to motivate learners. It can also lead to their withdrawing from the learning process in areas where they have been made to feel they are 'no good'. Motivation can be preserved and enhanced by assessment methods which protect the learner's autonomy, provide some choice and constructive feedback, and create opportunity for self-direction.

Principle 7: Assessment for learning should promote commitment to learning goals and a shared understanding of the criteria by which they are assessed

For effective learning to take place learners need to understand what it is they are trying to achieve – and want to achieve it. Understanding and commitment follows when learners have some part in deciding goals and identifying criteria for assessing progress. Communicating assessment criteria involves discussing them with learners using terms that they can understand, providing examples of how the criteria can be met in practice and engaging learners in self-assessment.

Principle 8: Assessment for learning should ensure that learners receive constructive guidance about how to improve

Learners need information and guidance in order to plan the next steps in their learning. Teachers should: pinpoint the learner's strengths and advise on how to develop them; be clear and constructive about any weaknesses and how they might be addressed; provide opportunities for learners to improve upon their work.

Principle 9: Assessment for learning should develop the learner's capacity for self-assessment so that they can become reflective and self-managing

Independent learners have the ability to seek out and gain new skills, new knowledge and new understandings. They are able to engage in self-reflection and to identify the next steps in their learning. Teachers should equip learners with the desire and the capacity to do this for themselves through developing the skills of self-assessment.

Principle 10: Assessment for learning should recognise the full range of achievements of all learners

Assessment for learning should be used to enhance all learners' opportunities to learn in all areas of educational activity. It should enable all learners to achieve their best and to have their efforts recognised.

Appendix 2
The Teaching and Learning Research Programme (TLRP): 10 principles of effective pedagogy (Teaching and Learning Research Programme 2007)

TLRP's evidence-informed principles are the product of an iterative process of consultation and debate between researchers, practitioners, policy-makers and the TLRP Directors' Team. It should be noted that these are in a continuous process of development.

1. Effective pedagogy equips learners for life in its broadest sense. Learning should aim to help individuals and groups to develop the intellectual, personal and social resources that will enable them to participate as active citizens, contribute to economic development and flourish as individuals in a diverse and changing society. This means adopting a broad conception of worthwhile learning outcomes and taking issues of equity and social justice for all seriously.

2. Effective pedagogy engages with valued forms of knowledge. Pedagogy should engage learners with the big ideas, key skills and processes, modes of discourse, ways of thinking and practising, attitudes and relationships, which are the most valued learning processes and outcomes in particular contexts. They need to understand what constitutes quality, standards and expertise in different settings.

3. Effective pedagogy recognises the importance of prior experience and learning. Pedagogy should take account of what the learner knows already in order for them, and those who support their learning, to plan their next steps. This includes building on prior learning but also taking account of the personal and cultural experiences of different groups of learners.

4. Effective pedagogy requires learning to be scaffolded. Teachers, trainers and all those, including peers, who support the learning of others, should provide activities, cultures and structures of intellectual, social and emotional support to help learners to move forward in their learning. When these supports are removed the learning needs to be secure.

5. Effective pedagogy needs assessment to be congruent with learning. Assessment should be designed and implemented with the goal of achieving maximum validity both in terms of learning outcomes and learning processes. It should help to advance learning as well as determine whether learning has occurred.

6. Effective pedagogy promotes the active engagement of the learner. A chief goal of learning should be the promotion of learners' independence and autonomy. This involves acquiring a repertoire of learning strategies and practices, developing positive learning dispositions, and having the will and confidence to become agents in their own learning.

7. Effective pedagogy fosters both individual and social processes and outcomes. Learners should be encouraged and helped to build relationships and communication with others for learning purposes, in order to assist the mutual construction of knowledge and enhance the achievements of individuals and groups. Consulting learners about their learning and giving them a voice is both an expectation and a right.

8. Effective pedagogy recognises the significance of informal learning. Informal learning, such as learning out of school or away from the workplace, should be recognised as at least as significant as formal learning and should therefore be valued and appropriately utilised in formal processes.

9. Effective pedagogy depends on the learning of all those who support the learning of others. The need for lecturers, teachers, trainers and co-workers to learn continuously in order to develop their knowledge and skill, and adapt and develop their roles, especially through practice-based enquiry, should be recognised and supported.

10. Effective pedagogy demands consistent policy frameworks with support for learning as their primary focus. Organisational and system level policies need to recognise the fundamental importance of continual learning – for individual, team, organisational and system success – and be designed to create effective learning environments for all learners.

Appendix 3
James and Pedder's (2006) hypotheses on assessment for learning

1. The collaborative engagement of teachers and students in assessment for learning processes makes methods and means of learning an explicit and critical focus of classroom interaction and enquiry among students and between students and teachers.
2. Through engagement in such explicit and interactive processes, teachers are able to help students develop their own and one another's increasing independence in diverse learning situations, including formally examined courses of learning. This and the previous characteristic are crucial classroom conditions necessary for helping students develop the sustainable skills and dispositions for learning how to learn in formal educational contexts.
3. Authentic assessment for learning is grounded in the sustained and critical reflection of teachers and students with regard to their preferences and processes, and the values and beliefs that gain their expression in them.
4. The quality of teaching and learning is enhanced in all situations where the assessment for learning methods that are used in classrooms are clearly and explicitly leveraged by, or developed out of, a set of values and beliefs about learning and teaching, which themselves are the focus for dialogue and enquiry in both classroom lessons and other learning contexts.
5. The implication for teachers' professional learning is that opportunities need to be designed and maximised to enable teachers to examine critically the values and beliefs that they consider shape their current practice. In so far as such learning opportunities clarify for individuals and groups of teachers where the key gaps are between their values and practices, teachers' learning can be focused in very practical ways to implement more values-informed classroom practices.

References

Adey, P, Robertson, A and Venville, G (2002) Effects of a cognitive acceleration programme on Year 1 pupils, *British Journal of Educational Psychology* 72, 1–25.

Alexander, R J (2012) *Visions of Education, Roads to Reform: the global educational race and the Cambridge Primary Review*, paper delivered at Universidad Gabriela Mistral, Santiago, Chile, 30 October 2012.

Anton, M (2012) Dynamic assessment, in Fulcher, G and Davidson, F (Eds) *The Routledge Handbook of Language Testing*, London: Routledge, 106–119.

Arter, J (1999) Teaching about performance assessment, *Educational Measurement: Issues and Practice* 18, 30–44.

Ashton, K, Salamoura, A and Diaz, E (2012) The BEDA impact project: A preliminary investigation of a bilingual programme in Spain, *Research Notes* 50, 34–41.

Assessment Reform Group (1992) *Policy Issues in National Assessment*, BERA Dialogues No 7, Clevedon: Multilingual Matters.

Assessment Reform Group (1999) *Assessment for Learning: Beyond the Black Box*, Cambridge: University School of Education.

Assessment Reform Group (2002) *Assessment for Learning: 10 Principles*, Cambridge: University School of Education.

Ausubel, D P (1968) *Educational Psychology: A Cognitive View*, New York: Holt, Rinehart and Winston.

Bachman, L F and Palmer, A S (1996) *Language Testing in Practice*, Oxford: Oxford University Press.

Bennett, R E (2011) *Formative assessment: A critical review*, paper presented at the Hong Kong Institute of Education, Hong Kong, SAR, China, 22 July 2010.

Bereiter, C and Scardamalia, M (no date) *What Will It Mean To Be An Educated Person in Mid-21st Century?* available online: www.gordoncommission.org/rsc/pdf/bereiter_scardamalia_educated_person_mid21st_century.pdf

Black, P (1993) Assessment policy and public confidence: comments on the BERA Policy Task Group's article 'Assessment and the improvement of education', *The Curriculum Journal* 4, 421–427.

Black, P and Wiliam, D (1998a) Assessment and classroom learning, *Assessment in Education* 5 (1), 7–73.

Black, P and Wiliam, D (1998b) *Inside the Black Box*, available online: weaeducation.typepad.co.uk/files/blackbox-1.pdf

Black, P and Wiliam, D (2003) 'In praise of educational research': Formative assessment, *British Educational Research Journal* 29 (5) 623–637.

Black, P and Wiliam, D (2009) Developing the theory of formative assessment, *Educational Assessment, Evaluation and Accountability* 21 (1), 5–31.

Black, P, Harrison, C, Lee, C, Marshall, B and Wiliam, D (2003) *Assessment for Learning: Putting it into Practice*, Maidenhead: Open University Press.

Bloom, B S (1969) Some theoretical issues relating to educational evaluation, in Tyler, R W (Ed) Educational evaluation: New roles, new means, *The 68th*

Yearbook of the National Society for the Study of Education Part II, Chicago: University of Chicago Press, 26–50.

Bond, T G and Fox, C M (2001) *Applying the Rasch Model*, Hillsdale: Lawrence Erlbaum Associates.

Boud, D (2000) Sustainable assessment: Rethinking assessment for the learning society, *Studies in Continuing Education* 22 (2), 151–167.

Boud, D and Falchikov, N (2006) Aligning assessment with long term learning, *Assessment & Evaluation in Higher Education* 31 (4), 399–413.

Brindley, G (2001) Outcomes-based assessment in practice: Some examples and emerging insights, *Language Testing* 18, 393–407.

Brindley, G and Burrows, C (Eds) (2001) *Studies in Immigrant English Language Assessment Volume 2*, Sydney: National Centre for English Language Teaching and Research, Macquarie University.

Broadfoot, P (1996) Assessment and learning: power or partnership? in Goldstein, H and Lewis, T (Eds) *Assessment: Problems, Developments and Statistical Issues*, Chichester: John Wiley & Sons, 21–40.

Broadfoot, P (2005) Dark alleys and blind bends: Testing the language of learning, *Language Testing* 22, 123–141.

Broadfoot, P and Black, P (2004) Redefining assessment? The first ten years of Assessment in Education, *Assessment in Education* 11 (1), 7–26.

Bronfenbrenner, U (1979) *The Ecology of Human Development: Experiments by Nature and Design*, Cambridge: Harvard University Press.

Brookhart, S M (1999) Teaching about communicating assessment results and grading, *Educational Measurement: Issues and Practice* 18, 5–13.

Brookhart, S M (2003) Developing measurement theory for classroom assessment purposes and uses, *Educational Measurement: Issues and Practice* 22 (4), 5–12.

Brown, J D and Hudson, T (1998) The alternatives in language assessment, *TESOL Quarterly* 32 (4), 653–675.

Butler, R (1987) Task-involving and ego-involving properties of evaluation: Effects of different feedback conditions on motivational perceptions, interest and performance, *Journal of Educational Psychology* 79 (4), 474–482.

Butler, R (1988) Enhancing and undermining intrinsic motivation: The effects of task-involving and ego-involving evaluation on interest and performance, *Journal of Educational Psychology* 58 (1), 1–14.

Butler, R and Neuman, O (1995) Effects of task and ego-achievement goals on help-seeking behaviours and attitudes, *Journal of Educational Psychology* 87, 261–271.

Butterfield, E C and Nelson, G D (1989) Theory and practice of teaching for transfer, *Educational Technology Research and Development* 37 (3), 5–38.

Bygate, P, Skehan, P and Swain, M (Eds) (2001) *Researching Pedagogic Tasks: Second Language Learning, Teaching and Testing*, Harlow: Pearson.

Cambridge English (2013) *Principles of Good Practice: Quality Management and Validation in Language Assessment*, Cambridge: Cambridge English Language Assessment.

Candlin, C (1987) Towards task-based language learning, in Candlin, C and Murphy, D (Eds) *Language Learning Tasks*, Englewood Cliffs: Prentice-Hall, 5–22.

Carless, D (2007) Learning-oriented assessment: Conceptual bases and practical implications, *Innovations, Education and Teaching International* 44 (1), 57–66.

Carless, D (2008) Developing productive synergies between formative and summative assessment processes, in Hui, M F and Grossman, D (Eds) *Improving Teacher Education Through Action Research*, New York: Routledge, 9–23.

Carless, D (2009) Learning-oriented assessment: Principles and practice and a project, in Meyer, L, Davidson, S, Anderson, H, Fletcher, R, Johnston, P M and Rees, M (Eds) *Tertiary Assessment & Higher Education Student Outcomes: Policy, Practice & Research*, Wellington: Ako Aotearoa, 79–90.

Chapelle, C (2009) The relationship between second language acquisition theory and computer-assisted language learning, *The Modern Language Journal 93,* 741–753.

Cheah, Y M (1998) The examination culture and its impact on literacy innovations: The case of Singapore, *Language and Education* 12, 192–209.

Clahsen, H and Felser, C (2006) Grammatical processing in language learners, *Applied Psycholinguistics* 27, 3–42.

Coleman, J A (2004) Modern languages in British universities: Past and present, *Arts and Humanities in Higher Education* 3, 295–317.

Council of Europe (2001) *Common European Framework of Reference for Languages: Learning, Teaching, Assessment*, Cambridge: Cambridge University Press.

Council of Europe (2002) *Guide for the development and implementation of curricula for plurilingual and intercultural education*, document prepared for the Policy Forum 'The right of learners to quality and equity in education – The role of linguistic and intercultural competences', Geneva, Switzerland, 2–4 November 2010.

Council of Europe (2010) *Guide for the Development and Implementation of Curricula for Plurilingual and Intercultural Education*, Strasbourg: Council of Europe.

Creswell, J W and Plano Clark, V L (2011) *Designing and Conducting Mixed Methods Research* (2nd edition), Thousand Oaks: Sage.

Csizer, K and Dörnyei, Z (2005) Language learners' motivational profiles and their motivated learning behavior, *Language Learning* 55 (4), 613–659.

Cumming, A (2009) Language assessment in education: Tests, curricula, and teaching, *Annual Review of Applied Linguistics* 29, 90–100.

Cumming, J J and Maxwell, G S (2004) Assessment in Australian schools: Current practice and trends, *Assessment in Education* 11, 89–108.

Daugherty, R, Black, P, Ecclestone, K, James, M and Newton, P (2008) Alternative perspectives on learning outcomes: Challenges for assessment, *Curriculum Journal* 19 (4), 243–254.

Davison, C (2007) Views from the chalkface: School-based assessment in Hong Kong, *Language Assessment Quarterly* 4, 37–68.

Davison, C and Hamp-Lyons, L (2009) The Hong Kong Certificate of Education: School-based assessment reform, in Cheng, L-Y and Curtis, A (Eds) *Hong Kong English Language Education*, London: Routledge, 248–266.

Davison, C and Leung, C (2009) Current issues in English language teacher based assessment, *TESOL Quarterly* 43 (3), 393–415.

Department for Education and Employment/Qualifications and Curriculum Authority (1999) *The National Curriculum Handbook*, London: Department for Education and Employment.

Dewey, J (1915) *The School and Society*, New York: Cosimo Classics.

Dewey, J (1916) *Democracy and Education*, New York: Free Press.

Dewey, J (1933) *How We Think*, available online: archive.org/details/howwethink000838mbp

Dewey, J (1938) *Logic: Theory of Inquiry*, available online: archive.org/details/JohnDeweyLogicTheTheoryOfInquiry

Dewey, J and McLellan, A (1908) *What Psychology Can Do for the Teacher*, New York: D Appleton and Company.

Dörnyei, Z (2006) Individual differences in second language acquisition, *AILA Review* 19, 42–68.

Dweck, C (1989) Motivation, in Lesgold, A and Glaser, R (Eds) *Foundations for a Psychology of Education*, Hillsdale: Lawrence Erlbaum Associates, 87–136.

Dweck, C (2000) *Self-theories: Their Role in Motivation, Personality and Development*, Philadelphia: Psychology Press.

Ellis, N C (1998) Emergentism, connectionism and language learning, *Language Learning* 48 (4), 631–664.

Ellis, N C (2012) Frequency-based accounts of second language acquisition, in Gass, S M and Mackey, A (Eds) *The Routledge Handbook of Second Language Acquisition*, Abingdon: Routledge, 193–210.

Ellis, R (1994) *The Study of Second Language Acquisition*, Oxford: Oxford University Press.

Ellis, R and Barkhuizen, G (2005) *Analyzing Learner Language*, Oxford: Oxford University Press.

Entwistle, N J and Entwistle, A C (1991) Forms of understanding for degree examinations: The pupil experience and its implications, *Higher Education* 22, 205–227.

European Commission (2012) *First European Survey on Language Competences: Final Report,* Luxembourg: Publications Office of the European Union, available online: eceuropaeu/languages/eslc/index.html

European Commission (2015) *Study on Comparability of Language Testing in Europe: Final Report 2015*, Luxembourg: Publications Office of the European Union.

Evans, J (2007) The emergence of language: A dynamical systems account, in Hoff, E and Shatz, M (Eds) *Handbook of Language Development*, Malden: Blackwell, 128–148.

Feldt, L S and Brennan, R L (1989) Reliability, in Linn, R L (Ed) *Educational Measurement* (3rd edition), New York: Macmillan, 105–146.

Filipović, L and Hawkins, J A (2013) Multiple factors in second language acquisition: The CASP model, *Linguistics* 51 (1), 145–176.

Frederiksen, J R and Collins, A (1989) A systems approach to educational testing, *Educational Researcher* 18 (9), 27–32.

Frederiksen, N, Mislevy, R J and Bejar, I (Eds) (1993) *Test Theory for a New Generation of Tests*, Hillsdale: Lawrence Erlbaum Associates.

Fredriksson, U and Hoskins, B (2007) *Indicators of Learning to Learn*, paper presented to ASLO project seminar, London, March 2007.

Fulcher, G (2010) *Practical Language Testing*, London: Routledge.

Fullan, M (1993) *Change Forces: Probing the Depths of Educational Reform,* London: The Falmer Press.

Fullan, M (1999) *Change Forces: The Sequel*, London: The Falmer Press.

Gardner, R C (1985) *Social Psychology and Second Language Learning: The Role of Attitudes and Motivation*, London: Edward Arnold.

Gass, S M (2003) Input and interaction, in Doughty, C J and Long, M H (Eds) *Handbook of Second Language Acquisition*, Malden: Blackwell, 224–255.

Gass, S M and Selinker, L (2008) *Second Language Acquisition: An Introductory Course* (3rd edition), New York: Routledge.

Gell-Mann, M (1992) Complexity and complex adaptive systems, in Hawkins, J A and Gell-Mann, M (Eds) *The Evolution of Human Languages*, Redwood City: Addison-Wesley, 3–18.

Geranpayeh, A and Taylor, L (Eds) (2013) *Examining Listening: Research and Practice in Assessing Second Language Listening*, Studies in Language Testing volume 35, Cambridge: UCLES/Cambridge University Press.

Gitomer, D H and Duschl, R A (2007) Establishing multilevel coherence in assessment, *Yearbook of the National Society for the Study of Education* 106 (1), 288–320.

Green, A (2007) *IELTS Washback in Context: Preparation for Academic Writing in Higher Education*, Studies in Language Testing volume 25, Cambridge: UCLES/Cambridge University Press.

Green, A (2012) *Language Functions Revisited: Theoretical and Empirical Bases Across the Ability Range*, English Profile Studies volume 2, Cambridge: UCLES/Cambridge University Press.

Hambleton, R K, Swaminathan, H and Rogers, H J (1991) *Fundamentals of Item Response Theory Volume 2,* Newbury Park: Sage.

Harlen W (2004) *A Systematic Review of the Evidence of the Impact on Students, Teachers and the Curriculum of the Process of using Assessment by Teachers for Summative Purposes,* available online: eppi.ioe.ac.uk/cms/Default.aspx?tabid=119

Harlen, W (2005) Teachers' summative practices and assessment for learning – tensions and synergies, *The Curriculum Journal* 16 (2), 207–223.

Harlen, W (2009) Improving assessment *of* learning and *for* learning, *Education 3–13: International Journal of Primary, Elementary and Early Years Education* 37 (3), 247–257.

Harlen, W and Deakin Crick, R (2002) *A Systematic Review of the Impact of Summative Assessment and Tests on Students' Motivation for Learning,* available online: eppi.ioe.ac.uk/eppiwebcontent/reel/review_groups/assessment/ass_rv1/ass_rv1.pdf

Harlen, W and James, M (1997) Assessment and Learning: differences and relationships between formative and summative assessment, *Assessment in Education: Principles, Policy & Practice* 4 (3), 365–379.

Harlen, W and Malcolm, H (1996) Assessment and testing in Scottish primary schools, *The Curriculum Journal* 7, 247–257.

Harlen, W, Gipps, C, Broadfoot, P and Nuttall, D (1992) Assessment and the improvement of education, *The Curriculum Journal* 3, 215–230.

Hattie, J (2005) *What is the Nature of Evidence that Makes a Difference to Learning?* available online: research.acer.edu.au/cgi/viewcontent.cgi?article=1008&context=research_conference_2005

Hawkey, R (2006) *Impact Theory and Practice: Studies of the IELTS test and Progetto Lingue 2000,* Studies in Language Testing volume 24, Cambridge: UCLES/Cambridge University Press.

Hawkins, J A and Buttery, P (2009) Using learner language from corpora to profile levels of proficiency: Insights from the English Profile Programme, in Taylor, L and Weir, C J (Eds) *Language Testing Matters: Investigating the Wider Social and Educational Impact of Assessment*, Studies in Language Testing volume 31, Cambridge: UCLES/Cambridge University Press, 158–175.

Hawkins, J A and Filipović, L (2012) *Criterial Features in L2 English: Specifying the Reference Levels of the Common European Framework*, English Profile Studies volume 1, Cambridge: UCLES/Cambridge University Press.

Hawkins, J A and Gell-Mann, M (Eds) (1992) *The Evolution of Human Languages*, Menlo Park: Addison-Wesley.

Hudson, T (2012) Standards-based testing, in Fulcher, G and Davidson, F (Eds) *Routledge Handbook of Language Testing*, London: Routledge, 479–494.

Huerta-Macías, A (1995) Alternative assessment: Responses to commonly asked questions, *TESOL Journal* 5 (1), 8–11.

Inbar-Lourie, O (2008) Constructing a language assessment knowledge base: A focus on language assessment courses, *Language Testing* 25 (3), 385–402.

Inhelder, B and Piaget, J (1958) *The Growth of Logical Thinking*, London: Routledge and Kegan Paul.

Ivanič, R (2004) Discourses of writing and learning to write, *Language and Education* 18 (3), 220–245.

James, M and Brown, S (2005) Grasping the nettle: Preliminary analysis and some enduring issues surrounding the improvement of learning outcomes, *The Curriculum Journal* 16 (1), 7–30.

James, M and Pedder, D (2006) Beyond method: assessment and learning practices and values, *The Curriculum Journal* 17 (2), 109–138.

James, W (1890) *The Principles of Psychology*, New York: Holt.

Johnston, P, Guice, S, Baker, K, Malone, J and Michelson, N (1995) Assessment of teaching and learning in literature-based classrooms, *Teaching and Teacher Education* 11, 359–371.

Jonassen, D and Land, S (Eds) (2012) *Theoretical Foundations of Learning Environments*, London: Routledge.

Jones, N (1992) *An item bank for testing English language proficiency: using the Rasch model to construct an objective measure*, unpublished PhD, University of Edinburgh.

Jones, N (2012) Reliability and dependability, in Fulcher, G and Davidson, F (Eds) *The Routledge Handbook of Language Testing*, London: Routledge, 350–362.

Jones, N (2013) The European Survey on Language Competences and its significance for Cambridge English Language Assessment, *Research Notes* 52, 2–7.

Jones, N (2014) *Multilingual Frameworks: The Construction and Use of Multilingual Proficiency Frameworks*, Studies in Language Testing volume 40, Cambridge: UCLES/Cambridge University Press.

Jones, N (2016) Intercultural competence – learning, teaching and assessment, in Docherty, C and Barker, F (Eds) *Language Assessment for Multilingualism: Proceedings of the ALTE Paris Conference, April 2014*, Studies in Language Testing volume 44, Cambridge: UCLES/Cambridge University Press, 17–27.

Jones, N and Saville, N (2007) Scales and frameworks, in Spolsky, B and Hult, F M (Eds) *The Handbook of Educational Linguistics*, London: Wiley-Blackwell, 495–509.

Jones, N, Saville, N and Hamilton, M (2013) *A systemic view of assessment within an educational context*, paper presented at ILTA/AAAL symposium, March 2013.

Keenan, E L and Comrie, B (1977) Noun phrase accessibility and universal grammar, *Linguistic Inquiry* 8 (1), 63–99.

Khalifa, H and Saville, N (2016) The impact of language assessment, in Tsgari, D and Banerjee, J (Eds) *Handbook of Second Language Assessment*, Berlin: Walter de Gruyter GmbH, 77–94.

Khalifa, H and Weir, C J (2009) *Examining Reading: Research and Practice in Assessing Second Language Reading*, Studies in Language Testing volume 29, Cambridge: UCLES/Cambridge University Press.

Khalifa, H, Nguyen, T and Walker, C (2012) An investigation into the effect of intensive language provision and external assessment in primary education in Ho Chi Minh City, Vietnam, *Research Notes* 50, 8–19.

Klein, W (1986) *Second Language Acquisition*, Cambridge: Cambridge University Press.

Kluger, A N and DeNisi, A (1996) The effects of feedback interventions on performance: a historical review, a meta-analysis, and a preliminary feedback intervention theory, *Psychological Bulletin* 119, 254–284.

Krashen, S (1982) *Principles and Practice in Second Language Acquisition*, Oxford: Pergamon.

Kulik, J A and Kulik, C-L C (1989) Meta-analysis in education, *International Journal of Educational Research* 13, 221–340.

Lantolf, J P and Poehner, M (2011) Dynamic assessment in the classroom: Vygotskian praxis for second language development, *Language Teaching Research* 15, 11–33.

Larsen-Freeman, D (1997) Chaos/complexity science and second language acquisition, *Applied Linguistics* 18 (2), 141–165.

Larsen-Freeman, D (2012) Complexity theory, in Gass, S M and Mackey, A (Eds) *The Routledge Handbook of Second Language Acquisition*, Abingdon: Routledge, 73–87.

Larsen-Freeman, D and Cameron, L (2008) *Complex Systems in Applied Linguistics*, Oxford: Oxford University Press.

Lave, J and Wenger, E (1991) *Situated Learning: Legitimate Peripheral Participation*, Cambridge: Cambridge University Press.

Learning and Teaching Scotland (2006) *Assessment Is for Learning Programme*, available online: www.gov.scot/Publications/2006/09/15090146/1

Lee, N and Schumann, J (2005) *The interactional instinct: The evolution and acquisition of language*, paper presented at AILA, Madison, Wisconsin.

Lepper, M R and Hodell, M (1989) Intrinsic motivation in the classroom, in Ames, C and Ames, R (Eds) *Research on Motivation in the Classroom Volume 3*, San Diego: Academic Press, 73–105.

Leung, C and Lewkowicz, J (2006) Expanding horizons and unresolved conundrums: Language testing and assessment, *TESOL Quarterly* 40 (1), 211–234.

Linn, R L, Baker, E and Dunbar, S B (1991) *Complex, Performance-based Assessment: Expectations and Validation Criteria*, available online: www.cse.ucla.edu/products/evaluation/cresst_ec1992_1.pdf

Lynch, B (2001) Rethinking assessment from a critical perspective, *Language Testing* 18 (4) 351–372.

Maloch, B (2002) Scaffolding student talk: One teacher's role in literature discussion groups, *Reading Research Quarterly* 37 (1), 94–112.

Mansell, W (2010) *The Assessment Reform Group: 21 Years of Investigation, Argument and Influence*, Cambridge: Cambridge Assessment Network.

Mansell, W, James, M and the Assessment Reform Group (2009) *Assessment in Schools. Fit for purpose? A Commentary by the Teaching and Learning Research Programme*, available online: www.tlrp.org/pub/documents/assessment.pdf

Marton, F, Hounsell, D J and Entwistle, N J (Eds) (1984) *The Experience of Learning*, Edinburgh: Scottish Academic Press.

McNamara, T (1996) *Measuring Second Language Performance*, London: Longman.

Messick, S (1989) Validity, in Linn, R L (Ed) *Educational Measurement* (3rd edition), New York: American Council on Education and Macmillan, 1–103.

Messick, S (1996) Validity and washback in language testing, *Language Testing* 13 (3), 241–256.

Milanovic, M and Saville, N (1996) *Considering the impact of Cambridge EFL examinations*, Cambridge: Cambridge ESOL internal report.

Mislevy, R J (1994) *Can There Be Reliability Without "Reliability"?* Princeton: Educational Testing Service.

Mislevy, R J (2004) Can there be Reliability without "Reliability?" *Journal of Educational and Behavioral Statistics* 29 (2), 241–244.

Mislevy, R J, Steinberg, L S and Almond, R G (1999) *Evidence-Centered Assessment Design*, Princeton: Educational Testing Service, available online: www.education.umd.edu/EDMS/mislevy/papers/ECD_overview.html

Moeller, A J, Creswell, J W and Saville, N (Eds) (2016) *Second Language Assessment and Mixed Methods Research*, Studies in Language Testing volume 43, Cambridge: UCLES/Cambridge University Press.

Moss, P A (2003) Reconceptualising validity for classroom assessment, *Educational Measurement: Issues and Practice* 22 (4), 13–25.

Murray, D (Ed) (2008) *Planning Change, Changing Plans: Innovations in Second Language Teaching*, Ann Arbor: University of Michigan Press.

National Research Council (2003) *Understanding Others, Educating Ourselves: Getting More from International Comparative Studies in Education*, Washington DC: The National Academies Press, available online: www.nap.edu/openbook.php?isbn=0309088550

New Zealand Qualifications Authority (no date) *Assessment and Examination Rules and Procedures for Secondary Schools,* available online: www.nzqa.govt.nz/about-us/our-role/legislation/nzqa-rules/assessment-including-examination-rules-2016/secondary-schools-supporting-information/

Norris, J M (2009) Task-based teaching and testing, in Long, M and Doughty, C (Eds) *Handbook of Language Teaching*, Cambridge: Blackwell, 578–594.

Norris, J M (2015) Thinking and acting programmatically in task-based language teaching: Essential roles for program evaluation, in Bygate, M (Ed) *Domains and Directions in the Development of TBLT: A Decade of Plenaries from the International Conference*, Amsterdam: John Benjamins, 27–58.

North, B (2000) *The Development of a Common Framework Scale of Language Proficiency*, New York: Peter Lang.

Nunan, D (1989) *Designing Tasks for the Communicative Classroom*, Cambridge: Cambridge University Press.

Nunan, D (2007) Standards-based approaches to the evaluation of ESL instruction, in Cummins, J and Davison, C (Eds) *International Handbook of English Language Teaching: Part One*, New York: Springer, 421–438.

O'Grady, W (2005) *Syntactic Carpentry: An Emergentist Approach to Syntax*, Hillsdale: Lawrence Erlbaum Associates.

Pellegrino, J W, Chudowsky, N and Glaser, R (2001) *Knowing What Students Know: The Science and Design of Educational Assessment*, Washington, DC: National Academy Press.

Perkins, D N and Salomon, G (1989) Are cognitive skills context-bound? *Educational Researcher* 18 (1), 21–26.

Perrenoud, P (1998) From formative evaluation to a controlled regulation of learning processes: Towards a wider conceptual field, *Assessment in Education: Principles, Policy and Practice* 5 (1), 85–102.

Phelps, R (1998) The demand for standardized student testing, *Educational Measurement: Issues and Practice* 17, 5–23.

Piaget, J (1976) *The Grasp of Consciousness*, Cambridge: Harvard University Press.

Poehner, M (2008) Both sides of the conversation: The interplay between mediation and learner reciprocity in dynamic assessment, in Lantolf, J and Poehner, M (Eds) *Sociocultural Theory and the Teaching of Second Languages*, London: Equinox Publishing, 33–56.

Poehner, M and Lantolf, J (2005) Dynamic assessment in the language classroom, *Language Teaching Research* 9 (3), 233–265.

Pollitt, A and Ahmed, A (2004) *Quantifying Support: Grading achievement with the support model*, paper presented at the IAEA Conference, Philadelphia, June 2004, available online: www.cambridgeassessment.org.uk/images/109718-quantifying-support-grading-achievement-with-the-support-model.pdf

Popham, W J (2008) *Classroom Assessment: What Teachers Need to Know* (5th edition), Boston: Pearson Allyn & Bacon.

Prabhu, N S (1987) *Second Language Pedagogy Volume 20*, Oxford: Oxford University Press.

Queensland Studies Authority (2009) *PD Packages*, available online: www.qcaa.qld.edu.au/p-10/past-curriculum-documents/implementing-essential-learnings-standards/pd-packages

Ramaprasad, A (1983) On the definition of feedback, *Behavioral Science* 28, 4–13.

Rea-Dickins, P (2006) Currents and eddies in the discourse of assessment: A learning focused interpretation, *International Journal of Applied Linguistics* 16 (2), 163–188.

Rea-Dickins, P (2007) Classroom-based assessment: Possibilities and pitfalls, in Cummins, J and Davison, C (Eds) *The International Handbook of English Language Teaching Volume 1*, Norwell: Springer, 505–520.

Robson, C (2002) *Real World Research: A Resource for Social Scientists and Practitioner-Researchers*, London: Blackwell.

Rodgers, E M (2004) Interactions that scaffold reading performance, *Journal of Literacy Research* 36 (4), 501–532.

Rogoff, B (1997) Evaluating development in the process of participation: Theory, methods, and practice building on each other, in Amsel, E and Renninger, A (Eds) *Change and Development: Issues of Theory, Application, and Method*, Hillsdale: Lawrence Erlbaum Associates, 265–285.

Rohrer, D and Pashler, H (2010) Recent research on human learning challenges conventional instructional strategies, *Educational Researcher* 39 (5), 406–12.

Sadler, D R (1989) Formative assessment and the design of instructional systems, *Instructional Science* 18, 119–144.

Sadler, D R (1998) Formative assessment: Revisiting the territory, *Assessment in Education: Principles, Policy and Practice* 5, 77–84.

Sadler, D R (2007) Perils in the meticulous specification of goals and assessment criteria, *Assessment in Education: Principles, Policy & Practice* 14 (3), 387–392.

Salamoura, A, Docherty, C and Hamilton, M (2013) *The use of external standardised assessment in a school context for motivational and accountability purposes*, paper presented at the 35th Annual Language Testing Research Colloquium, 1–5 July 2013, Seoul, Korea.

Salamoura, A, Khalifa, H and Docherty, C (2014) *Investigating the impact of language tests in their educational context*, paper presented at IAEA conference, 2014.

Saussure, F D (1916) *Cours de linguistique générale*, London: Duckworth.

Saville, N (2003) The process of test development and revision within UCLES EFL, in Weir, C J and Milanovic, M (Eds) *Continuity and Innovation: Revising the Cambridge Proficiency in English Examination 1913–2002*, Studies in Language Testing volume 15, Cambridge: UCLES/Cambridge University Press, 57–120.

Saville, N (2009) *Developing a model for investigating the impact of language assessment within educational contexts by a public examination provider*, unpublished thesis, University of Bedfordshire.

Saville, N (2010) Developing a model for investigating the impact of language assessment, *Research Notes* 42, 2–8.

Saville, N (2012) Applying a model for investigating the impact of language assessment within educational contexts: The Cambridge ESOL approach, *Research Notes* 50, 4–8.

Sayer, A (1984) Defining the urban, *Geojournal* 9 (3), 279–284.

Sayer, A (1992) *Method in Social Science: A Realist Approach*, London: Hutchinson.

Sayer, A (2000) *Realism and Social Science*, London: Sage Publications.

Scott, D (1991) Issues and themes: Coursework and coursework assessment in the GCSE, *Research Papers in Education* 6, 3–19.

Sebba, J and Deakin Crick, R (2005) *Systematic Review of Research Evidence of the Impact on Students of Self and Peer Assessment*, available online: eppi.ioe.ac.uk/cms/Default.aspx?tabid=2415&language=en-US

Shavelson, R J (2008) Guest editor's introduction, *Applied Measurement in Education* 21 (4), 293–294.

Shavelson, R J (2009) *Reflections on learning progressions*, paper presented at the Learning Progressions in Science (LeaPS) Conference, June 2009.

Shaw, S and Weir, C J (2007) *Examining Second Language Writing: Research and Practice in Assessing Second Language Writing*, Studies in Language Testing, volume 26, Cambridge: UCLES/Cambridge University Press.

Shepard, L A (2000) The role of assessment in a learning culture, *Educational Researcher* 29 (7), 4–14.

Shepard, L A (2006) Classroom assessment, in Brennan, R L (Ed) *Educational Measurement* (4th edition), Westport: American Council on Education/Praeger, 623–646.

Shepard, L A (2008) Formative assessment: Caveat emptor, in Dwyer, C A (Ed) *The Future of Assessment: Shaping Teaching and Learning*, Hillsdale: Lawrence Erlbaum Associates, 279–303.

Shohamy, E (1997) *Critical language testing and beyond*, plenary talk presented at the American Association of Applied Linguistics (AAAL) Meeting, Orlando, Florida.

Simpson, M (1990) Why criterion-referenced assessment is unlikely to improve learning, *The Curriculum Journal* 1, 171–183.

Sjøberg, S (2007) Constructivism and learning, in Baker, E, McGaw, B and Peterson, P (Eds) *International Encyclopaedia of Education* (3rd edition), Oxford: Elsevier, available online: folk.uio.no/sveinsj/Constructivism_and_learning_Sjoberg.pdf

Skehan, P (1998) *A Cognitive Approach to Language Learning*, Oxford: Oxford University Press.

Slavin, R E (1987) Mastery learning reconsidered, *Review of Educational Research* 57, 175–213.

Spolsky, B (1995) *Measured Words: Development of Objective Language Testing*, Oxford: Oxford University Press.

Stiggins, R (1999) Evaluating classroom assessment training in teacher education programs, *Educational Measurement: Issues and Practice* 18, 23–27.

Stiggins, R (2008) *An Introduction to Student-involved Assessment for Learning* (5th edition), Upper Saddle River: Pearson.

Swain, M (1985) Communicative competence: Some roles of comprehensible input and comprehensible output in its development, in Gass, S and Madden, C (Eds) *Input in Second Language Acquisition*, Rowley: Newbury House, 235–253.

Swain, M (2001) Examining dialogue: another approach to content specification and to validating inferences drawn from test scores, *Language Testing* 18 (3) 275–302.

Taylor, L (2000) Stakeholders in language testing, *Research Notes* 2, 2–3.

Taylor, L (2009) Developing assessment literacy, *Annual Review of Applied Linguistics* 29, 21–36.

Taylor, L (Ed) (2011) *Examining Speaking: Research and Practice in Assessing Second Language Speaking*, Studies in Language Testing volume 30, Cambridge: UCLES/Cambridge University Press.

Teaching and Learning Research Programme (2007) *Principles into Practice*, available online: www.tlrp.org/findings/Schools%20Findings/Schools%20 Findings.html

Teaching and Learning Research Programme (2013) *Teaching and Learning Research Programme*, available online: www.tlrp.org

Teasdale, A and Leung, C (2000) Teacher assessment and psychometric theory: A case of paradigm crossing? *Language Testing* 17 (2), 163–184.

Thelen, E and Smith, L B (1994) *A Dynamic Systems Approach to the Development of Cognition and Action*, Cambridge: The MIT Press.

Truscott, J and Sharwood Smith, M (2004) Acquisition by procession: A modular perspective on language development, *Bilingualism: Language and Cognition* 7, 1–20.

Turner, C E (2006) Professionalism and high-stakes tests: Teachers' perspectives when dealing with educational change introduced through provincial exams, *TESL Canada Journal* 23 (2), 54–76.

Turner, C E (2012) Classroom assessment, in Fulcher, G and Davidson, F (Eds) *The Routledge Handbook of Language Testing*, Routledge: Oxford, 65–78.

Van den Branden, K (Ed) (2006) *Task-based Language Education: From Theory to Practice*, Cambridge: Cambridge University Press.

Van Geert, P (2007) Dynamic systems in second language learning: Some general methodological reflections, *Bilingualism: Language and Cognition* 10, 47–49.

VanPatten, B (1996) *Input Processing and Grammar Instruction*, Norwood: Ablex.

VanPatten, B (Ed) (2004) *Processing Instruction: Theory, Research and Commentary*, Hillsdale: Lawrence Erlbaum Associates.

VanPatten, B (2007) Input processing in adult second language acquisition, in VanPatten, B and Williams, J (Eds) *Theories in Second Language Acquisition*, Hillsdale: Lawrence Erlbaum Associates, 115–135.

VanPatten, B (2008) Processing matters, in Piske, T and Young-Scholten, M (Eds) *Input Matters*, Clevedon: Multilingual Matters, 47–61.

Vygotsky, L (1978) *Mind in Society*, Cambridge: Harvard University Press.

Vygotsky, L (1986) *Thought and Language*, Cambridge: MIT Press.

Watkins, C, Carnell, E, Lodge, L, Wagner, P and Whalley, C (2000) *Learning about Learning*, London: Routledge.

Weir, C J (2005a) Limitations of the Council of Europe's Framework of reference (CEFR) in developing comparable examinations and tests, *Language Testing* 22 (3), 281–300.

Weir, C J (2005b) *Language Testing and Validation: An Evidence-Based Approach*, Oxford: Palgrave.

Whiting, B, Van Burg, J W and Render, G F (1995) *Mastery learning in the classroom*, paper presented at the Annual Meeting of the AERA, San Francisco 1995.

Whittington, D (1999) Making room for values and fairness: teaching reliability and validity in the classroom context, *Educational Measurement: Issues and Practice* 18, 14–22.

Wiggins, G P (1993) *Assessing Student Performance*, San Francisco: Jossey-Bass.

Wiggins, G P (1998) *Educative Assessment. Designing Assessments To Inform and Improve Student Performance*, San Francisco: Jossey-Bass.

Wiggins, G P and McTighe, J (1998) *Understanding by Design*, Alexandria: Association for Supervision and Curriculum Development.

Wiliam, D (2006) *Assessment for learning: Why, what and how*, paper presented to the Cambridge Assessment Network, available online: www.dylanwiliam.org/ Dylan_Wiliams_website/Papers_files/Cambridge%20AfL%20keynote.doc

Wiliam, D and Black, P J (1996) Meanings and consequences: A basis for distinguishing formative and summative functions of assessment? *British Educational Research Journal* 22, 537–554.

Wilson, B G and Myers, K M (2000) Situated cognition in theoretical and practical context, in Jonassen, D and Land, S (Eds) (2012) *Theoretical Foundations of Learning Environments*, London: Routledge, 57–88.

Withers, G (1987) From marking strategy to assessment procedure: A review of recent Australian practices, *Studies in Educational Evaluation* 13, 7–19.

Wood, D, Bruner, J S and Ross, G (1976) The role of tutoring in problem solving, *Journal of Child Psychology and Psychiatry* 17 (2), 89–100.

Wright, B D and Stone, M H (1979) *Best Test Design*, Chicago: MESA Press.

Xu, X and von Davier, M (2006) *Cognitive Diagnosis For NAEP Proficiency Data*, available online: onlinelibrary.wiley.com/doi/10.1002/j.2333–8504.2006. tb02014.x/abstract

Author Index

Subject Index

Lightning Source UK Ltd.
Milton Keynes UK
UKOW06f0815100516

273940UK00009B/261/P